Madonna Revealed

MADONNA

Revealed

The Unauthorized Biography

by Douglas Thompson

A BIRCH LANE PRESS BOOK
Published by Carol Publishing Group

A Birch Lane Press Book
Published by Carol Publishing Group
Birch Lane Press is a registered trademark of Carol Communications, Inc.

Editorial Offices: 600 Madison Avenue, New York, N.Y. 10022
Sales & Distribution Offices: 120 Enterprise Avenue, Secaucus, N.J. 07094
In Canada: Musson Book Company, a division of General Publishing Company, Ltd.,
   Don Mills, Ontario M3B 2T6

Queries regarding rights and permissions should be addressed to Carol
Publishing Group, 600 Madison Avenue, New York, N.Y. 10022

Carol Publishing Group books are available at special discounts for bulk
purchases, for sales promotions, fund raising, or educational purposes.
Special editions can be created to specifications. For details contact:
Special Sales Department, Carol Publishing Group, 120 Enterprise Avenue,
Secaucus, N.J. 07094

Manufactured in the United States of America
10   9   8   7   6   5   4   3   2   1

Library of Congress Cataloging-in-Publication Data

Thompson, Douglas
      Madonna revealed : the unauthorized biography / by Douglas
Thompson.
         p.   cm.
      "A Birch Lane Press book."
      ISBN 1-55972-099-9
      1. Madonna, 1959-   . 2. Rock musicians—United States—
Biography. I. Title.
ML420.M1387T5   1991
782.42166'092—dc20
      [B]   91-34976
                                                      CIP
                                                      MN

To Lesley for her love, patience, and Dandy

Contents

	Acknowledgments	ix
	Prologue: The Greatest Show on Earth	1
1.	Roots	5
2.	Sexual Beginnings	15
3.	Sexual Adventures	25
4.	Cheap Popcorn	33
5.	April in Paris	41
6.	The Experts	47
7.	The Movies	55
8.	Romantics	67
9.	Another Day, Another Brawl	79
10.	Jailhouse Blues	89
11.	Madonnamania	97
12.	Bad Memories	105
13.	The Top of the Hill	119
14.	Breathless	129
15.	The Charmer	135
16.	Madonna Inc.	141
17.	Leather and Lace	151
18.	Hooray for Hollywood	165
	Epilogue: Alone on the Hill	177

ACKNOWLEDGMENTS

Madonna tries to conceal herself with her own version of Great Britain's Official Secrets Act. All of her employees must sign contracts swearing not to reveal *anything* about her or her life-style. Thankfully, secrecy pacts are made to be broken, and my thanks goes to the many who did talk. Also to the Hollywood community from the nightclub doormen to the studio chiefs—everybody has a story or opinion about Madonna.

Special thanks for help and encouragement to Angela Miller and to Jeanne Karas, the diligent, digging fact-finder in Los Angeles.

I do think someone is protecting me. I don't know if it's an angel. It could be the Devil. —Madonna in 1990

Madonna Revealed

Prologue: The Greatest Show on Earth

The dazzling gown was like another of her snakeskins. You expected her to slither out of it at any second. It shimmered. She shimmied.

No one had ever worked the Oscars—or the ceremony's one billion television viewers worldwide—with the brassy bravado of platinum-blond Madonna. She did a bump and grind wearing twenty million dollar's worth of a girl's best friend. The diamonds twinkled even against the competition of her pearl-encrusted lethally low-cut dress.

The veterans ogled and said she'd brought the glamour back to

1

Hollywood and its annual cavalcade of self-acclaim—with a bang. And with the roll of a hip and the thrust of a buttock. If she'd performed like that in the street she'd have been arrested rather than grandly and most approvingly applauded.

She sang the Oscar-nominated Stephen Sondheim song "Sooner or Later (I Always Get My Man)" from the film *Dick Tracy*. She ignited and then fanned the flames of the torch song. The song won an Academy Award. Sizzling Madonna won the evening.

She'd made her appearance on stage through backstage magic— an elevator lift from the orchestra pit—to gasps from the celebrity-crowded audience. Her mock strip routine was a wow, especially when she turned her rear end to the crowd and simply wiggled. Even Madonna's high-profile "date," Michael Jackson, in his gold-tipped cowboy boots, took second place to the entertainer, who, on Monday, March 25, 1991, at the Shrine Auditorium in downtown Los Angeles, appeared on stage as more like Marilyn Monroe than Monroe.

The sixty-third Annual Academy Awards celebrated one hundred years of film. The traffic started jamming up around the Shrine Auditorium around 4:00 P.M. The Shrine holds sixty-two hundred people—twice as many as the Dorothy Chandler Pavilion, longtime home of the Oscars. More people but less class. There were lines of limousines, formally dressed men, and carefully coiffed and gowned women, but they were serving hot dogs and snacks, and wine in paper cups on what is supposedly Hollywood's champagne and caviar night. This was tacky in Tinseltown.

By 6:00 P.M. at the Shrine the atmosphere was decidedly down-at-heel. The excitement level measured a zero on the Richter scale. Then came a seismic roar from the crowds in the bleachers.

Madonna had arrived.

With Michael Jackson.

The tinsel was back in town. Madonna waltzed her way into the Awards as though she owned them. The pearls on her white gown played laser games with popping flashbulbs. Photo opportunity? No, this was paparazzi heaven.

Inside, Madonna and Jackson, both in white and bejeweled, took the two front-row aisle seats center stage. Throughout the auditorium people craned their necks to get a better look. Dustin Hoffman stood up to see what was going on. *Dick Tracy* costar Al Pacino waved. *Everyone* wanted Madonna's attention. Later, during a commercial break and away from the television cameras, master of ceremonies Billy Crystal peered down from the stage at Madonna and inquired: "Who do you have to fax to get on the show." Ironically, it was the same evening that Kevin Costner and his *Dances With Wolves* rode off with seven Oscars. The good guys won.

But so did the Bad Girl.

The entertainment world's commercial chameleon had just performed to her biggest audience *ever*. And it was a captive audience. Satellites in the sky had beamed her backside to the world's television audience. She'd shaken it at them. A superconfident superstar?

Probably only from the front-row seats at the Shrine where you could see close up and "live" could you also see the private shakes. Watching from there you could see that Madonna was as nervous as anyone might be performing on such an evening. Madonna nervous? Oh, yes. For despite her backside-to-the-world image, this is a still-insecure multimillionairess. She still does not have all that she wants. Every bump and grind on Oscar night had been rehearsed again and again and again by this perfectionist performer.

She's determined to be the best. To be the boss. To be in total control. Madonna Louise Veronica Ciccone is determined. Period. It's in her genes.

1

Roots

Io sono fiera di essere italiana [I'm proud to be an Italian].—Madonna to sixty-five thousand Italian fans at Florence's football stadium in 1987

Gaetano Ciccone was nineteen. His new bride, Michelina, was a year younger. They were living with his family in the easygoing community of Pacentro at the foot of Mount Amaro in central Italy. It was 1919, the First World War was over, and the world was changing. In Pacentro, it was for the worse. The people were farmers. They were also poor. But it was a pleasant place to live. Families left their doors unlocked. There was no crime. There was also no work or the prospect of it in Milan in the north or in Rome to the west.

A short, wiry, and determined man, Gaetano Ciccone had to make a decision for himself, his bride, and the babies they talked about having. He wanted lots of sons. She wanted daughters. They both wanted a good life. They had to emigrate or starve. For Gaetano Ciccone, who is remembered in Pacentro as a feisty, driven character, there was no choice.

5

America, the New World, was a magnet for the poor of Europe. It offered so much. Those who had gone and returned did so in style. Between 1920 and 1930, there were 455,315 Italian immigrants to the United States, and that was despite the Immigration Act of 1924, which assigned Italians an annual quota of only 3,845 immigrants. In 1920, Gaetano and Michelina Ciccone were two of them. They arrived in America with only a couple of battered suitcases. They could speak no English.

They had made the trek from Pacentro to Sulmona and then the 186 miles from there to Naples by foot. It was a dusty and hungry trip, but they were young and strong. Emotionally, it was more torturous. They were leaving the stability of their home and families, and investing their hopes, their very lives, in an alien culture and country. It was a gamble, a chance to profit by risk.

The voyage from Naples to New York on the SS *Regina d'Italia* of the Lloyd Sabaudo line took eleven weeks. The Ciccones were in steerage, which meant sleeping on deck in chafing saltwater-damp blankets.

On April 29, 1920, the *Regina d'Italia* entered Upper New York Bay and sailed on past the Statue of Liberty and the final three-quarters of a mile toward Ellis Island. Gaetano and Michelina Ciccone were up close to the rails along with all the other passengers. Their eyes dazzled as they stared out at their new land and unknown future.

The *Regina d'Italia* anchored at quarantine. Inspectors and immigration officials boarded to survey the latest delivery from crowded Europe. The passengers were many, the formalities swift. Along with the others the Ciccones were put on barges and ferried to Ellis Island. All those who have walked down the gangplank and up the quay to the New World can recall the noise of the ground-floor baggage room. It was in every way a Babel. And above the smell of the masses there was the welcome aroma of thick soups, stews, and freshly baked bread. Medical and legal examinations took place in the Great Hall upstairs. The Ciccones waited on wooden benches for their turn, manifest tags with two numbers attached to their worn coats. They were each asked thirty questions in two minutes. In English. "What is your name?" "Where were you born?" An interpreter stood by as the Ciccones were quizzed in parrot fashion. "Are you an anarchist?" "Do you have a criminal record?" "Do you have any skills?"

Gaetano Ciccone had no skills. He had strengths. He was able-bodied. He wanted "honest work" to support his family. This was still the time of the *padroni* at Ellis Island. These were labor bosses who spoke Italian and English and who understood the ways of the Old World and the needs of the New World. They had contacts with industrial concerns throughout New York, New Jersey, Pennsylvania, and southern New England.

By this time, mutual benefit societies had replaced the extended families of the Italian villages like Pacentro, which today is home to only 1,496 people. In 1920, "Sons of Italy" had 125,000 members in 887 lodges across America. The sons helped with sickness, despair, and death; it was a means of providing inexpensive group insurance.

When, on May 1, 1920, the Ciccones officially stepped onto American soil, Prohibition, the law that was to lead to turbulent times, to the Roaring Twenties, had just gone into effect. The Eighteenth Amendment and the Volstead Act, both effective as of January 26, 1920, launched great groups of Italian Americans as crime entrepreneurs. At the same time, the rise of Mussolini and Fascism in Italy forced many Mafia leaders to make a trip similar, if more comfortable, to that of the Ciccones. English was bastardized: vischi (whiskey) was what the ghengas (gangs) were selling on the strittos (streets).

The immigrants loved the music halls, which were free (the profits came from liquor sales), and the opera. Cleofante Campanini was the first conductor and director of the Metropolitan Opera House. Giulio Gatti Casazza was its general manager from 1908 to 1934. The Italian cultural overhaul of the New World was well in progress. So was the popular one—Frank Sinatra, Dean Martin, and Tony Bennett would all become musical legends.

Gaetano Ciccone, being interviewed on Ellis Island, looked around in bewilderment. But he heard the words "hard work" and "best pay," and he understood them. He and his wife decided to go to Pittsburgh, an inland port and one of the world's greatest steel centers and headquarters to some of America's biggest corporations. There were ferries to transport the newcomers one mile to Manhattan or the mere three hundred yards to the piers of New

Jersey where most immigrants settled. But, again, Gaetano Ciccone decided on the longer journey and the greater risk in hope of greater profit.

The days in Pittsburgh started early and finished late. The Ciccones worked hard. They moved into a rented one-bedroom house near the steel mill in a very poor, but proud, Little Italy ghetto. They didn't need to learn English—everyone spoke Italian. Gaetano Ciccone got his dearest wish—sons. Six of them. And he raised them Old World style. As the father, he was the interpreter of all their needs and interests. His authority was total and he maintained it by strict discipline. It was the same for all the families. Children were given responsibility at an early age. Daughters did not work: they prepared for marriage at home and were expected to marry the spouses chosen by their parents. But things were changing in the New World. In 1919, a study in New York showed that 91 percent of girls over fourteen were working for wages—and in turn, of course, were also acquiring an independence unknown in the Old Country.

But in Pittsburgh, Gaetano Ciccone ruled his house old-time style. The aim was to keep the family unit together. Five of his sons went into the steel mills. Silvio "Tony" Ciccone was the youngest and most doted upon of the six. The "baby" of the family, he went to college and got a degree in engineering. There were no openings for optic and defense engineers in a steel town when he graduated. Short and wiry and in other ways like his father, he left the stability of home and moved to where the work was: Detroit.

Silvio Ciccone wanted to better himself. He was of the New World, but he was also his father's son. Discipline, honesty, and hard work were the creed. Integrity was the byword: teach by example. The Catholic church provided a helpful rule book as a guide. Silvio had never wanted for a necessity, but as the youngest of a poor immigrant family, he'd had a hand-me-down upbringing. It's easy to understand his deep need to provide, and provide well. And that meant having the confidence not to follow the herd. Clever and inventive, he put in the hours at several car companies in the Detroit area, in the city that would become famous for the Motown—Motor Town—sound. And, later, for another anything-but-assembly-line product.

When Silvio Ciccone was called up for the armed services, he was skilled enough to join the air force—you *had* to join the air force: they *put* you in the army or navy. He was a straight shooter and well liked. Another airman in his group, Michael Fortin, also came from Michigan, and they traveled back from a Georgia posting together. After the war, Fortin introduced Silvio Ciccone to his youngest sister—a stunning looking woman named Madonna.

The two fell hopelessly in love at first sight.

A French-Canadian, Madonna Fortin was born in Bay City, a chill of a place on Lake Huron's Saginaw Bay. And that's were Silvio Ciccone went to visit with her family.

Following his stint in the air force Silvio had left the Chrysler Corporation and gone to work for General Dynamics. There was a postwar boom—the motor industry sold 9.3 million cars in 1955, and suburban housing tracts were changing the life-style aspirations of the working and middle classes. These were the days of the American dream of happy families—the stereotype was television's "Father Knows Best" with Robert Young—a television and a garage with two cars. Marriage seemed a perfectly wonderful idea. The full-scale white wedding took place in a church in Rochester, Michigan, which was then a new and developing community, not the urban sprawl it is today. Then as now, many of the smaller cities were lumped together as "Detroit."

In 1957, with Eisenhower in the White House, Ciccone's first son Anthony was born. A year later Martin arrived. The following summer another child was due. The family wanted to escape the overbearing heat that comes up and off the Great Lakes in July and August. Silvio Ciccone took the family north to stay with his in-laws in Bay City.

The legend-to-be was born on August 16, 1959, a hot, sunny day when the only clouds in the sky were man-made ones from the factories and chemical dumps. It was a remarkably easy birth. The Ciccone's first daughter seemed anxious to get on with her life.

The world was changing. Castro had taken control in Cuba. John F. Kennedy was on his way to the White House. Without Evita, Juan Peron had been overthrown in Argentina. Antonioni's then avant-garde *L'Avventura* was being filmed. Jack Kerouac had published *On the Road*. Americans were being told they didn't have to conform, and that message was circling the world.

And another nonconformist had joined it.

The day Madonna Louise Veronica Ciccone was born, Elvis Presley was atop the American pop charts with "A Big Hunk O' Love," having knocked Paul Anka's "Lonely Boy" from the number-one spot. It was an important week for Elvis, who was serving with the U.S. Army in Germany—he was introduced to fourteen-year-old Priscilla Beaulieu, the daughter of an army captain, who would become his wife and part of the Elvis legend.

This was the news the Ciccones heard on the radio and read in the *Rochester Eccentric,* the local newspaper, while baby Madonna rolled around in diapers. How could they have imagined that in not so many years their bald baby daughter's name would be as well known around the world as the King's?

Madonna was obviously named after her mother—but it was not an obvious thing to do. It marked her as something special from the start: it was rare for the matriarch of an Italian-Catholic family to pass on her name, especially such an exotic one with all of its religious implications.

The Ciccone's annual birth pattern continued. Madonna's sister Paula was born in 1960, then Christopher and Melanie. Six kids. One salary. Tough, but for Silvio Ciccone possible.

I think my earliest memories go back to about four or five years old and they're memories of my beautiful mother. They're really great memories. When I was four and younger, I remember not being able to sleep at night. I would walk to my parents' bedroom and push the door open. They were both asleep in bed and I think I must have done this a lot, gone in there, because they both sort of sat up in bed and said, "Oh no, not again." and I said: "Can I get into bed with you?"

I always went to sleep right away when I slept with them. I felt really lonely and forlorn even though my brothers and sisters were in my room with me. I wanted to sleep with my parents.

I remember, because my mother had a really beautiful red nightgown, silky red. My father was against me getting into bed with them and I remember getting into bed and rubbing against her nightgown and going to sleep—just like that.

To me that was heaven, to sleep between my parents.

What happened next was to tear Madonna's young life apart and brand and mold her future. Nearly thirty years later, she is still dealing with it and regularly seeing a woman psychiatrist in Beverly Hills.

Madonna's mother died of breast cancer at the age of thirty. Madonna was six. A couple of years later her father remarried. Madonna felt abandoned by one parent and betrayed by the other. A lost little girl. It's in her work, in her videos and songs. She will live with it forever. One friend, Lori Jahns, told me that even when they were out on wild dates, her "best friend" Madonna—Lori called her "Mud" and they wrote affectionate letters to each other for several years—would often grow quiet and say, "I miss my mother."

Years later, Madonna keeps a photograph of her mother in a silver frame on an antique night table in the bedroom of her art-filled home at the top of the Hollywood Hills. The art she owns is worth millions, but the snapshot of a sixteen-year-old dark-haired girl in a long, white dress is priceless. Another favorite picture is of herself, aged seven, wearing her mother's wedding gown and veil.

The death goes on hurting Madonna. It is always in her words:

When I see my girlfriends with their mothers even now I can't even imagine—it's unfathomable what that sort of nurturing would have done for me. I really miss it. My role models who nurtured me when I was growing up were all men. It's true. Life is just too short and I have too many goddamn things to do, so I better hurry up. That has a lot to do with my mother's death—I've felt that way since I was a child. I think the biggest reason I was able to express myself and not be intimidated was not having a mother. Women are traditionally raised to be subservient, passive, accepting. The man is supposed to be the pioneer. He makes the money, he makes the rules. I know that some of my lack of inhibition comes from my mother's death. For example, mothers teach you manners. And I absolutely did not learn any of those rules and regulations.

She watched her mother waste away from breast cancer. It took a year, an agonizing one of futile treatments, painkillers, and then the morphine-induced hazy, hanging-on days until the end. Of any subject—and she's proved she's not afraid of any—this is the one where Madonna finds most eloquence for her emotions:

I remember her being a very forgiving, angelic person. I have a memory of my mother in the kitchen scrubbing the floor. She did all the housekeeping and she was always picking up after us. We were really messy, awful kids. I remember having these mixed feelings. I have a lot of feelings of love and warmth for her, but sometimes I think I tortured her. I think little kids do that to people who are really good to them. They can't believe they are not getting yelled at or something so they taunt you. I really taunted my mother. I remember, I also knew she was sick for a long time with breast cancer so she was very weak, but she would continue to go on and do things she had to do. I knew she was very fragile and getting more fragile.

I knew that because she would stop during the day and just sit down on the couch. I wanted her to get up and play with me and do the things she did before. I know she tried to keep her feelings inside and not let us know. She never complained. I remember she was really sick and was sitting on the couch. I went up to her and I remember climbing on her back and saying, "Play with me, play with me," and she wouldn't. She couldn't and she started crying and I got really angry with her, pounding her back and saying, "Why are you doing this?" Then I realized she was crying.

I remember feeling stronger than she was. I was so little and I put my arms around her and I could feel her body underneath me sobbing and I felt like she was the child. I stopped tormenting her after that.

She spent about a year in the hospital and I saw my father going through changes. He was devastated. It was awful to see your father cry. But he was very strong about it. He would take us to the hospital to see her and I remember my mother was always cracking up and making jokes. She was really funny so it wasn't so awful going to visit her there.

Then my mother died. I remembered that right before she died she asked for a hamburger. She wanted to eat a hamburger because she couldn't eat anything for so long and I thought that was very funny. I didn't actually watch her die.

Then everything changed.

And so, Madonna says, had she. "That was the turning point. The die was cast. I think that made me grow up fast. I knew I could be either sad or take control and say, 'It's going to get better.'"

After his wife's death, Silvio Ciccone was forced to separate his family for a time. It was crushing—the patriarch was meant to keep his family together. But how could he work and care for his children? The solution came some months later in hiring a housekeeper. This brought the children back together. They had one housekeeper, then another, and another. The children's behavior was wild—a throwback to their easygoing mother. "I think my parents pissed a lot of people off because they had so many kids and they never screamed at us. My older brothers were rambunctious and they would start fires in the basement or throw rocks at windows and my mother and father would never yell at them. They would just hug us and wrap their arms around us and talk to us quietly."

It was a cozy time before death intruded. Madonna recalls her father's "integrity"—she didn't agree with all his Old World values or, when it came to that, some of the New World ones either—and his living by example.

A lot of parents tell their kids not to smoke cigarettes and they smoke cigarettes. Or they give you some idea of sexual modesty—but my father lived that way. He believed that making love to someone is a very sacred thing and it shouldn't happen until after you are married. He stuck by those beliefs and that represented a very strong person to me. He was my role model. I was my father's favorite. I knew how to wrap him around my finger. I knew there was no other way to go besides saying, "No, I'm not going to do it." I employed those techniques. I was a very good student. I got all A's. My father rewarded us for good grades. He gave us quarters and fifty cents for every A we got. I was really competitive and my brothers and sisters hated me for it. I made the most money every report card. I'd pit myself against all of them. It wasn't because I was going to learn; it was only to be the best. Of course, all my brothers and sisters wanted to beat me up.

She could handle that. But the piano! Her father made all the children learn a musical instrument and take a daily lesson. She took piano. She hated it. She convinced her father with those young wiles to allow her to take dance lessons, tap and jazz, and baton twirling. She says these classes were hangouts for hyperactive girls.

And Madonna had to cope with equally rowdy brothers who would hang her up on the clothesline by her underwear. She says she always talked out of turn, and her sister Paula, a tomboy, and the boys would gang up on her. She ratted on them to their father. He was Daddy Dearest. But he also brought the news that wrecked her world and still shakes it today. The tension among those trying to get on with living was at times intolerable.

"My father told me my mother was dead, but you keep waiting for her to come back. We never all sat down and talked about it. I guess we should have." Her mother's death turned Madonna into a preteen basket case, totally dependent on her father. She would be physically sick when he left the house for longer than it took to put out the garbage. She was frightened he too would leave. She thought she had cancer. She would creep into her father's bed every night. "I kept telling him that if he ever died, I was going to be buried in the casket with him. He would say, 'Don't talk like that—that's really disgusting.'" What *she* found utterly disgusting was his decision to marry again.

And after her father's decision to remarry, Madonna took a peculiar revenge. Even she doesn't know where her mind was then, but she decided she would never again visit her mother's grave. For the time, she wanted to be Cinderella. She reneged on this warped decision—but not until 1990.

_2_

Sexual Beginnings

"Papa Don't Preach"—The second single from Madonna's 1986 album _True Blue_

Madonna and her brothers and sisters never took to their housekeepers. Who could replace their mother? Madonna felt she too would die young. There was loneliness, a longing just for something; later she would call it "an emptiness—if I hadn't had that, I would never have been so driven." There was also fear. There were stairs in her house with spaces between the steps. She thought the Devil was in the basement and would always dash up the stairs so he wouldn't grab her by the ankles. Illogical, yes, but although she was scared, she still scooted up those stairs.

Madonna was not so quick to react to the demands of the housekeepers who seemed to spin through her home as though they were on a merry-go-round. Women, small and tall, big and trim, young and middle-aged—but all strangers. It was hard to accept discipline from strangers: wash the dishes, tidy the room, make the bed, and on an on in a domestic litany. But there was one whom the kids liked, Angelica Roberts, who resembled Natalie Wood.

15

Their father married another one of the housekeepers, Joan Stone. Madonna now had to compete with another woman for her father's attention. And then there were more babies. Her half sister Jennifer was born in 1968, and, back on the annual cycle, Mario was born the following year.

They all lived in a two-story colonial home just off Old Perch Road in Rochester in a little court of homes called Oklahoma. Madonna was the oldest girl. She took care of business—and that was mostly changing the babies' diapers. It was a torturous time, but also character building, and either good or bad depending on your viewpoint. Her father insisted on church before parochial school every day. After school, the uniform came off and there were jobs around the house. There was homework, dinner, and no television except for the Saturday morning cartoons. The rest of TV was sinful. The family never went out to the movies or out to dinner. Magazines were a luxury. This period was like the winding of a spring in preparation for the drive and energy Madonna would need to achieve so much fame and fortune in less than a decade. It was also the birth of the Madonna style—or lack of it.

Her father insisted the children call his new wife "Mother" or "Mom." But to Madonna Michelle was her "stepmother," and she could do no right. Madonna was not allowed to use tampons because her stepmother said they were the equivalent of sexual intercourse. To avoid arguments, all the girls were bought similar dresses. Madonna hated to look like her sisters, and she detested the uniform required by her Catholic schools. She put bows in her hair and would wear razzle-dazzle socks. Her secret joke was the brightly colored underpants she wore instead of the regulation dark blue ones. It didn't stay a secret for long—the children would tease each other by lifting up their skirts: most girls were mortified. Madonna retaliated with an unexpected flash of pink or black-and-white polka dots. If no one lifted her skirt for her, teachers recall she regularly took solo action during recess, hanging upside down on the playground monkey bars to reveal her rainbow of underwear.

Madonna desperately wanted to be the oddball. Her brother Martin, now a gleaming, curly-haired, good-looking disc jockey with a Detroit radio station recalls, "She wasn't rich, she wasn't famous then, but she was the same girl—always being different from the others." She was closest to her brother Christopher, who is now an interior designer in Los Angeles: "In an Italian home, socializing always centered around the kitchen so Madonna and I both know the value of a good pot to make a big batch of pasta." Both brothers remember Madonna as always seeking attention: climbing onto tables and dancing at family get-togethers. She would hurt herself, burn her fingers on the stove—just to get attention.

By the age of ten Madonna had turned into a precocious little flirt. She was socializing outside the family circle and was by now adept at getting herself noticed. She had long dark hair, a winning smile, and a sweet look. This was the beginning of the glossy veneer and incredible play acting that would finally result in the self-sustaining phenomenon of Madonna, The Act.

The family attended St. Andrews Church in Rochester and Madonna went to the Holy Family Regional School which was, and is, a rather foreboding looking building on the outskirts of town. Today things are not so strict, but current headmistress Mrs. Sylvia Trepanier laughs, "I'm not sure we would want to acknowledge Madonna as a former pupil."

And that was true as much in the past as it is today. Ten-year-old Madonna was a terror. Ask Tommy, the child with bad teeth whom she chased around the playground. Madonna really went after her young man. Once she tore off her school blazer and white blouse and went topless after him. One of the nuns grabbed her and furiously explained that little girls did not take off their clothes and chase boys.

Until that moment Madonna had been obsessed with becoming a nun. She thought they were so special, so very beautiful. "I saw them as really pure, disciplined, sort of above average people. They never wore any makeup and they had these really serene faces. Nuns are sexy." Of course, they didn't chase boys. Madonna's career goals at the time were to become a nun or a movie star. Looking back, she says just nine months of convent school put her well off the first idea. But not off Tommy ("I wanted him"). The day after the playground chase, she received her first kiss. From Tommy. In the convent. Today, she still recalls the moment as "incredible." Madonna's first kiss in a convent. Well, what else?

It was the start of the rebellion. And her sexual revolution:

"Probably about the same time as I began to rebel against the church I went through puberty. That was when I really started to think about sex, about its presence, not about what I was going to do about it."

Carol Belanger, who was in the Brownies with Madonna, recalls the convent days, the interest in sex—and in what the nuns had beneath their habits: "Madonna and I went peeking through the windows of the convent to see the nuns without their habits. We found out they had hair." Belanger, who is married and still lives in the Rochester area, often attended church with Madonna. Once they went naked—under their coats. As they sat through the services, they exchanged knowing glances and suppressed giggles.

School friends remember Madonna as the girl who was willing to take all the risks. If there were apples to steal, she'd lead the group. When they went on shoplifting sprees, she would regularly get away with the most loot. She even wore pants to church, which her father hated.

Madonna's first great public dare was at St. Andrews' annual talent show. She was in the seventh grade, but a fast-developing twelve-year-old. The parishioners gathered early in the church hall. Fathers had come home early from the car factories, showered, and put on dress shirts and ties. Mothers were wearing their Sunday dresses. And most of the kids performing were in their Sunday best, reciting poetry or tap dancing or singing or playing the piano.

Madonna came on stage nude. Well, she looked naked. She was aping Goldie Hawn from the "Laugh-In" show of the sixties when Hawn used to gyrate her body which was adorned with only a skimpy bikini and paint. Silvio Ciccone's little girl wore green fluorescent paint and what could be mistaken for a monokini. The music started blasting—"Baba O'Reilly" by the Who. Under a black light and with a strobe light, Madonna wiggled and undulated and leaped about on stage. The only thing not moving were the parents' eyeballs. They were frozen in shock. The kids, especially the boys, were turned on by Madonna's first public performance. She had spent weeks planning her act, the costumes, the antics. Her father took thirty seconds to grab her as she left the stage. She was "grounded" for two weeks. She can smile about it now: "He was mortified. He just about dismembered me."

As she went into her teens, Madonna became wilder rather than tamer. And also more curious. About her body, about boys, about everything.

And there were also the other kids at school:

> You want to identify with somebody as you are growing away from being a child. You're starting to think differently and you want to be independent, but before you reach that independence you want to attach yourself to someone. In school there were hippies—the more *free* group, the guys with long hair who took a lot of jewelry and shop classes and smoked a lot of pot during lunch hour. I didn't identify with them because I thought they were extremely lazy. Then there was a jock group and they were drunk on beer every day. I was a cheerleader for a little while, but I couldn't get into it. It wasn't that I didn't like athletics—I couldn't get into the sensibilities of cheerleaders and athletes. They were only interested in sports, drink, and girls. I had this idea that everyone went to junior high and high school with blinders on their eyes and it really pissed me off. I was sure everyone was missing something and I wandered around aimlessly. My best friends were the guys who were really studious like physics majors.

But it wasn't easy being anybody's friend. The boys thought she was easy. The girls thought so too. An attractive blond called Katrina made her suspicions known after her boyfriend started flirting with Madonna. She slapped Madonna's face. On the street. In front of much of the school. Madonna was devastated. But not enough to slow down. She was listening to Diana Ross and the Supremes and to the young Stevie Wonder. Frankie Lymon's songs made her weak in the knees. And she would let everyone know what she thought. "Sometimes I literally put my hand over her mouth to shut her up," says Carol Belanger. "A group of bikers once dropped firecrackers on us. Madonna yelled at them and told them to knock it off. One of the biker girls came down and started hitting her in the mouth. We finally got away, but she had a black eye and a bruised cheek."

At home, Silvio Ciccone still ran a strict ship. Madonna had to go to a friend's house to watch TV shows like "Dark Shadows" and

"The Monkees," and to drool over David Cassidy in "The Partridge Family."

Madonna fought with her father, mostly about religion. She would find ways to pretend she was going to a different Mass than he was and then take off with her friends. She always thought ahead and worked out the "sermon" she had heard to stop being caught out by her father if he quizzed her.

Since the Rochester public school system had a better reputation than Madonna did on the Holy Family school playground, Silvio Ciccone decided to take his oldest daughter out of the Catholic school and send her to Rochester West Junior High.

Madonna wanted to be "European." She stopped shaving her legs and her armpits, and wore gypsy-style clothes. Her new best friend was Lori Jahns. "Mud" Ciccone and Lori Johns developed together. Lori recalls:

> We were real close in eighth grade. She had other friends, but it was *us*. We sent letters back and forth and we'd call each other all the time—spend the night together if we could. I guess, back then, you always had a best friend. We had friendship rings and all that kind of jazz. She'd had a tough time at the Catholic school. Too strict. I guess the nuns were real bitches. They were just so strict and nasty and she would tell jokes about stuff they would try and get away with. That's why she was going nuts when she got to public school. For someone who had had to wear a uniform to school to just go to your closet and say "I wanna wear this!" was wonderful. Or to go to a friend's house and go: "Oh, I have twice the wardrobe now." Hot pants were big back then and those Godawful bell-bottom jeans, those hip-huggers. She loved to borrow clothes and stuff. If it's your best friend, then it's fine. The clothes she had weren't that great. I guess it wasn't as big a deal to her family as it was to some others.
>
> My mom didn't like her very much. She thought she'd lead me astray. She thought there was something different about her. She would never say why. Maybe it was because of her independence or because she was very headstrong. Her family was different from my family. My family always seemed to be close and dinnertime was when you sat down and chatted.

And it didn't seem that close at her house.

We were into boys, boys, and more boys. Girls mature quicker than guys and she wrote to me about two boys saying she wished they'd grow because they were so adorable. They were short and really cute but it was like, "Hmm, this doesn't look right."

We did a lot of boy talk and girl stuff. We'd sit around and sing. She would sing. Carole King was real big then and we'd sing her songs. I remember spending one night at her [Madonna's] house. It was the summer and we went for a walk. And then there was just all kinds of guys who would get together and practice music in someone's garage or basement. That was a big thing so they could play at high school dances. She knew a guy down the street and we went there dancing. They said, "Let's just goof around, why don't you guys sing backup?" I don't even know what song it was. It was "Proud Mary" or something like that. I didn't sing. I danced. And she got up and sang backup. She wasn't frightened at all.

She was fearful at times. She didn't get along well with her stepmother. Her father was doing two jobs. There was a new woman in their home getting Dad's attention.

Madonna was her mother's baby because she was the first girl. She seldom talked about it, and when she did, she was very emotional about it. Seeing her mom die had such an impact on her. She mentioned her mom's suffering and when she did talk about it she would always say, "I wish my mom were here." It was always sad. I couldn't pinpoint anything that started conversations like that. She must think about her mom all the time. I'm sure she does even now. About being a loner. She said it gave her commitment, she wanted to do something. She'd say, "Fine, I'm gonna do this. I *can* do this." I think that has a lot to do with her today. It was like her dancing. We did a talent show in the eighth grade and she wanted me to do this dance number with her. She choreographed it herself and everything and I still remember the song and the lyrics, "Let your body feel the music and feel the beat and just kind of groove to the music." I mean, she would just dance like you could not believe. She was loose. She could really do it.

Madonna didn't care what anybody thought. She was just being her own self. "I wanna do what I wanna do" was her motto. And that's what she eventually did.

Her father was one stickler for homework. You did your homework before you did anything else. She was very intelligent. I would have to study, study, study to get my B's and A's. I had to work a lot harder than she did to get the same results.

She shared a bedroom with her sisters Paula and Melissa then. A lot of times I'd ask her to come over to my house and she couldn't because she had to watch the little kids because her stepmom was doing something. Her father wasn't around much. He worked a lot of hours. It was a hard time for her. It was a development time. And she was a *lot* more developed than some of us. But she wasn't easy or a sleaze as we'd call it back then. I've read things that say she's had her boobs done and this and that. She never did. She always had a gorgeous figure.

Bisexual?

It raises a little controversy and gets people talking. But back at school, it was just boys as far as I know. But kids experiment.

The friends began going to catechism together.

I wasn't a Catholic. My mother asked, "Why do you want to go to catechism?" "It's interesting, Ma. You learn about different things." I learned about boys and so did Madonna.

That's when you're finding out your sexuality and everything else. We'd do a lot of heavy petting. In a sense there was peer pressure to be cool. But at the same time, we wanted to be our own individuals. And that's hard at that age when you're trying to find out what and who you are.

Rochester was a very small, beautiful town then. You wouldn't know it anymore. It's overdeveloped, the roads can't handle the traffic. When we all first lived there, there was the golf course and the cow pasture and we could ride our bikes and go to Baskin-Robbins for ice cream.

Or we would skip catechism and go to the movies. Of course, we sat there and kissed with the boys in the front row of the movie theater. Necking with the guys from catechism.

It was then that Madonna invented her "floozy" look. The girls knew their parents didn't like it and that made it even more fun. Madonna: "We got dressed to the nines. We got bras and stuffed them so our breasts were over-large and wore really tight sweaters—we were sweater-girl floozies. We wore tons of lipstick and really badly applied makeup and huge beauty marks and did our hair up like Tammy Wynette. We posed. We took turns lounging on the bed with our hands behind our head. We took pictures of each other and developed them and these were our ten-cent-floozy pictures."

Madonna the floozy moved to Rochester-Adams High School and her friend Lori Jahns went to Rochester High. They were rival cheerleaders.

But Madonna had solo flirtation and going-steady rights with big-smiling Nick Twomey who is now a Michigan pastor. And she developed her ongoing fascination with Marilyn Monroe, turning herself into a Monroe wannabe.

3

Sexual Adventures

> The only remotely entertainment-orientated dream I ever had was one where I dreamed I kissed Robert Redford. I was in the sixth grade. And it has not come true. —Madonna in 1990

The Reverend Nick Twomey is a neatly-dressed, dark-haired man with horn-rimmed glasses, a picture of propriety. He is pastor at the Faith Reformed Church in Traverse City, Michigan. He used to "go steady" with Madonna and they were friends until they both graduated from Rochester-Adams High School in 1976. She was a cheerleader. He played on the football, basketball, and baseball teams. "We did some serious flirting. We sort of hung out together," recalled the pastor. "You do that more, I suppose, than going steady in seventh, eighth, and ninth grade."

Neither of them belonged in the popular, mainstream crowd at school. He became a Christian. She took on her European look. They were different.

Even when we were no longer superclose, we had a mutual respect for one another because neither of us cared what the other kids thought. My life zigged, her life zagged.

We've all heard about her rebel life, but I'm not so sure she was *such* a rebel. Neither of us had halos on our heads, but I don't know that either one of us was any worse than the other.

I've thought about Madonna and I remember how she was. She was often confused. I wonder if she is happy. I suspect that underneath all the fame and fortune is a person in need of love, forgiveness, and hope.

In her teens Madonna was misunderstood. The boys would call her "a nympho" and the girls put her down as "a slut," but she was still a virgin. However, she was never one to wait to be asked for a date. If she liked a boy, she asked him out. She got a *reputation*. She was necking with the boys. And there was some heavy petting. She took precautions: to heavy necking parties, what they called "make-out" nights, she wore a turtle-necked blue bodysuit. No matter how hot it got, there were several zippers between her virginity and lusty teenaged boys. But teenagers, those hormones on two legs, are on a constant sexual voyage of discovery. Madonna couldn't go on forever being the girl who went to church every Sunday morning in a starched white dress and who knelt with her brothers and sisters, father, and stepmother in the third row from the front.

She lost her virginity in the back of a Cadillac. Later, she would regret describing it—in a joke that backfired—as a career move. But she didn't go "all the way" until she had been dating Russell Long for several months. He was two years older, drove that infamous Cadillac, and smoked marijuana. "I don't know if it was anything to do with me," says Russell. "I think it was more to do with adventure, of the experience of the unknown. She really wanted to find out what it was like."

Sex was now very much on her mind. She and her old Carol Belanger would joke about it—they even stripped Ken and Barbie and put them face-to-face under the covers of Barbie's bed. Madonna spent hours reading *Glamour* and *Seventeen* magazines. They gave her the sweater idea, a way to brighten up her school uniform by wearing hot pink, purple, and orange sweaters. She was never frightened of others laughing at her or jeering at her.

Most of us don't like to be stared at for being different, the odd one out. Madonna's strength in the playground—and now—is that she doesn't care what others think. She says she knew she was different from the age of five. So, having her first sexual experience was not because of peer pressure: it was simply because she wanted to see what it was like. She was fifteen. "The idea that the first guy I ever slept with is married and has kids really breaks me up. I wonder if he still loves me—he probably does."

But there were sexual adventures before that. In her 1991 documentary *Truth or Dare*, Madonna confronts the woman she says "finger-fucked" her when they both lived in Michigan. The woman in question couldn't recall the particular incident. Madonna counters, "All children experiment with each other sexually when they're little. These are things that people just want to sweep under the rug and treat like dark, dirty secrets, when they shouldn't be." And Madonna says that from her earliest sexual longings, she was attracted to *all* sides of sexuality. As with everything else in her life, she wanted to know *all* about it. In those growing-up years, Madonna did feel great pressure to "fit in," to be part of a group. You had to be a member of the church, a participant in neighborhood and school activities. That pressure made her angry. The escape was to dance to Motown records at her friends' homes. They would stack portable turntables with 45's, the Supremes, Martha and the Vandellas, the Shirelles, the Ronettes, and dance and sing. Oooooooohhh, baby love, and be-bop-de-bop. Madonna made up routines. The other kids would give her standing ovations and she liked the applause. Another pastime was to go to the movie theater that showed foreign and old movies. She saw flickering black and white films with Carole Lombard and Judy Holliday. And Brigitte Bardot and Marilyn Monroe. "She [Monroe] was my first movie idol. When I first saw her, I wanted to make my hair blonde and wear pointy bras."

Madonna saw herself in those screen sirens. Her humor, her need to be the boss, to be in control, and at the same time to be cared for. She was then the same paradox she is today. She had knowledge. She also had innocence. And years later, in December 1986, she would pose Monroe-style in the pages of *Life* magazine. And she would do it again, even more spectacularly on the cover and pages of *Italian Vogue* and worldwide editions of *Vanity Fair* in March 1991. She had "become" Marilyn for the camera. She posed and pouted like her idol, and a few weeks later she appeared at a Beverly Hills benefit concert in a short, black dress—a mirror of Monroe.

Psychologists have, and had, warned her about this obsession. But Madonna believes Monroe, whose mother was committed to an asylum soon after Monroe was born, rose above her difficult start in life. She is irritated when warned off the Monroe reincarnation track: "Marilyn Monroe was a victim and I'm not. I know what I'm doing and what I want. If I make mistakes or fall into traps, they're mine, not Marilyn Monroe's."

Madonna has a collection of Monroe memorabilia. In the videos for "Material Girl" and "Papa Don't Preach," she struts Monroe-style recalling her idol's hit films *Gentlemen Prefer Blondes* and *There's No Business Like Show Business.* She shrugs off stories that she consulted psychics who told her she was Monroe reincarnate. But it's a subject she's pursued since her mid-teens.

Madonna was the one to call on at school for a different take. In junior high, classmate Jonathan Gilbert decided to make a short 8mm film. He wanted a naked tummy on which to simulate frying an egg for his cameras. Madonna obliged.

By sixteen, dance had become her passion. Whenever touring dance companies visited the Detroit area, she would fight for tickets. She took every dance class she could. It was through dance that her teenage anger subdued. She had oriented herself. "I was a little girl from Michigan and I had a dream and I worked really hard and my dream came true." She wanted to dance seriously. And Christopher Flynn taught serious dance.

Flynn was forty-five when Madonna met him, a lean man with thinning hair and glasses. He was a homosexual and a Catholic. She adored him. Her family was not in the least worldly. Michigan is not America's most cultural state. It's a hard-working blue-collar place, and no more so than in Detroit and its suburbs. Flynn understood Madonna. She looked to him as a mentor, a father figure and even as an imaginary lover and brother. Lover, brother, and father—a trinity of people the seventeen-year-old felt she didn't have close to her. Flynn did not disguise his sexual preference. Instead, he took Madonna to gay discotheques in downtown Detroit. The crowd was doing "poppers" (capsules of amyl nitrate) and talking literature and poetry. They couldn't have been more different from all those school playground jocks whose lives revolved around sports, drinking, and girls. This was glamour. This was sophistication. What it was, of course, was new and different.

Flynn took Madonna to museums and art exhibitions in Detroit. And they would go dancing. Flynn was later to recall, "She was hot. People would clear the floor. But she's that way about life. She was always trying to be better, always positive, always filled with urgency, always wanting the most of it, and she had this tremendous thirst for everything. She was insatiable." Even for silly knock-knock jokes. Flynn remembered a two-hour drive in which she made them up one after the other, and he marveled, "They were good."

Madonna had graduated from Rochester High and won a dance scholarship to the University of Michigan, an achievement that had not thrilled her father. By then, she wore her hair in a short, spiky punk look. At the university there was discipline, including a tough plié exercise—low knee bends with the stomach held tightly in and the posture perfect. Madonna broke up the class one day during the exercise with a loud belch. On a hot day, she wanted to take off her leotards and just wear a bra, no bottoms. She hammed it up in ballet class. She ripped pieces out of her leotards and wore safety pins and scratched runs into her tights.

Flynn had told her she had a face like a Roman statue. She was extremely well built for her age with breasts that had the neighborhood boys goggle-eyed—something she did nothing to discourage. But Flynn told her she was beautiful. No one had said that before. Even Russell, in his moments of passion, had praised her body rather than her total look. She understood Flynn to mean that she was beautiful not only in appearance but inside. It was then that her mind took the step beyond fact, on to theory, and later to the fantasies she would capitalize on in her career. *Anything* was possible.

Madonna has no doubts about Flynn's influence:

I'd say that after my father, the most powerful, important relationship of my life was with Christopher Flynn. I didn't understand the concept of gay at that time. I was probably twelve or thirteen years old. All I knew was that my ballet teacher was different from everybody else. He was so alive. He had a certain theatricality about him. He made you proud of yourself—just they way he came up to me and put my face in his hand and said, "You are beautiful." No one had woken up that part of me yet. I was too busy being repressed by my Catholic father.

By the time I was fifteen or sixteen, he took me to my first gay club to go dancing. I'd never been to a club. I'd only been to high-school dances, and no guys would ever ask me to dance because they thought I was insane, so I'd just go out and dance by myself.

Flynn's gay world made her feel "normal." And she explains:

In school and in my neighborhood and everything, I felt like such an outsider, a misfit, a weirdo. And suddenly, when I went to the gay club, I didn't feel that way anymore. I just felt at home. I had a whole new sense of myself.

Until that point, I kept seeing myself through macho heterosexual eyes. Because I was a really aggressive woman, guys thought of me as a really strange girl. I know I frightened them. I didn't add up for them. They didn't want to ask me out. I felt inadequate around them, and I felt not beautiful, and I felt like I could never fit in with the prom queens and the cheerleaders and the perfect girls that all went out with the football players.

You can understand Flynn's attraction for this "misfit."

I was really down on myself. When Christopher introduced me to this life, I suddenly thought, "That's not the only way that I have to be." I felt that my behavior was accepted around him. My father didn't know. At the time, he would have freaked out.

People didn't talk about gay life in the Catholic church. They barely talked about sex. So I didn't see it as something I was supposed to be wary of or afraid of. All I knew was, I was attracted to Christopher and his life-style. I fell in love with him and the way he treated me. I started spending a lot of time with dancers, and almost every male dancer that I knew was gay. Then I went through another kind of feeling inadequate because I was constantly falling in love with gay men. Of course, I was so miserable that I wasn't a man.

But she had the "balls" to move on.

It was Christopher Flynn who encouraged Madonna to stretch, to move away, to try New York. Flynn died of AIDS at the Hernandez House hospice in Los Angeles on October 27, 1990. Madonna was distraught. A California newspaper contacted Flynn a few weeks before he died. He told them that he and Madonna had kept in touch: "We still remained friends after Madonna found her own way in life and achieved her dream. We had a special relationship. She was a very worldly sort of woman even when she was little more than a child."

Flynn had told her "New York." She told her father. He was against it. So was just about everybody else. But Flynn had told her she was beautiful, she could do it. She felt she was simply marking time at the University of Michigan's dance department, just tuning her technique. She dropped out and took a Northwest Airlines jet—her first plane ride—to New York. Her ticket cost her eighty-eight dollars.

4

Cheap Popcorn

I always meet certain people at certain times in my life who can help me.—Madonna in 1985

Michigan to Manhattan? It's a lot longer than the miles involved. Madonna was nearly nineteen. And budding. There was no hiding her figure—and she didn't try. And she didn't have any thoughts about the perils of the big city. She was totally self-absorbed and hardly noticed the other passengers on the jet. *She* was the one heading for New York City and the big time. If there were any regrets about her leaving her hometown, they belonged to Steve Bray. Some months earlier at the smoke-filled Blue Frogge night-club, a favorite of the University of Michigan's preppy crowd, Madonna had picked him up. She had been dancing up a storm and fighting off the attention of a crowd of students when Bray caught her eye. He was black. He was a waiter. He was funny. And more importantly—he was cool. Bray was also a gifted musician, a drummer with a local band that worked the Detroit lounge circuit. Bray—like so many in the years to come—was captivated by Madonna's energy and what he would later call her "aura of ambi-

33

tion." And it was that ambition which allowed her to leave Steve Bray, a man who would later come to have an enormous impact on her life and career, with hardly a thought about his feelings.

It was midsummer when Madonna landed at La Guardia Airport. Hot and sticky. She was carrying the dark blue winter coat that she couldn't fit into her suitcase, which was filled with her ballet shoes, tights, underwear, a couple of outfit changes, two pairs of street shoes, and a picture of her mother. She gathered her belongings together and, weighed down by her suitcase, made her way down the escalator and through the glass electric doors to the cab stand outside La Guardia's Northwest terminal.

She told the cab driver to take her to the middle of everything. She was lucky. The driver took her to Times Square and only wanted a dozen dollars for the trip. She walked east on Forty-second Street and then south on Lexington Avenue. There was one of those open-air summer markets going on Lexington. By now she was wearing her coat rather than carrying it. A man started following her. It looked as though all her father's predictions about coming to a nasty end in New York were coming true faster than even he could have believed. But the follower was no rapist or mugger—rather, a Good Samaritan. He quizzed her about why she was wearing a coat in the heat. She explained she was just off the plane and had nowhere to stay.

She stayed at this man's apartment for her first two weeks in New York with breakfast provided. He showed her the city and then she was off, to one cockroach-infested slum after another. She'd try to eat one apple a day, but mainly lived on popcorn. It was cheap. It filled her up. She also dined out of street trash cans. She'd look for the McDonald's bags because there were usually a few french fries in them. She was also adept at "borrowing" five dollars from every other man she met. She was sexually ambivalent to these men—come hither but go no further. "She was definitely not trampy, not free with her sexual favors," says Camille Barborne, Madonna's first manager and mentor. "She never lost her sense of pride. She always carried herself with a great deal of dignity."

She spent a long time living in a rooming house on Thirtieth Street between Eighth and Ninth avenues. Steve Bray and other friends recall the stench: vagrants peed or did worse in doorways.

She moved up to a place between Avenues A and B, and Bray, a gregarious, round-faced, and friendly character, says the smell there was better, but when he visited, "I always thought I was going to be killed by junkies."

New York, New York. Madonna gritted her teeth. She was a cloakroom girl at the trendy Russian Tea Room on West Fifty-Seventh. She was lonely. But there was nowhere else to go. She couldn't go home, could she? That would be defeat. She went to work for Dunkin' Donuts which had less of a jet-set crowd than the Tea Room. Seems some jam got squirted on a rather overbearing customer. She got fired. She couldn't drive (she finally got a California license in 1985 after a series of back-to-back lessons) so she'd dress up and just wander around the city with people gaping at her outlandish outfits. She would ride the subway enjoying all the attention. The Lower East Side of New York was her territory.

Madonna got a job slinging food at a Burger King just down from Central Park. The pay was $1.50 an hour. She found out art classes were paying ten dollars an hour for nude modeling. Madonna suddenly felt—financially and emotionally—rampantly artistic. Her body was in great shape, if a little underweight, from her popcorn diet. Her muscle definition and skeleton were on display for the student artists. She was their favorite model—she was easy to draw. She started modeling privately in people's homes. And that involved photographers. Her attitude was that Michelangelo wasn't a pornographer and neither were the artists and photographers she posed for.

And there were many, many modeling sessions from 1979 to 1980, more to put food on the table and pay the rent than for the artistic endeavor. Later, of course, as had happened to Marilyn Monroe before her, the nudes done back then would surface after she had become a worldwide phenomenon.

The pictures are now hot stuff. Back then they were just cold work. "It was cold in my studio," remembers photographer Martin Schreiber. "I had two heaters on Madonna but she was laughing." Schreiber founded the Photographing the Nude course at New York's New School. From February 10 through Valentine's Day in 1979 his students snapped away at a new model who their teacher called "a beautiful, intelligent, unconventional lady." He says now: "She was skinnier. There was something special about her, that's for sure. I think she's quite beautiful now, but she had a different kind of beauty then. I don't think she really knew what she wanted then, but she had some ideas.

"She was experimenting. She would do whatever it took to get to where she wanted to go."

Of the photographic sessions he said:

There was no hesitation on her part. "Here I am—it's no big deal." That was her attitude. With lots of nudes I don't photograph faces, but with her I wanted to include the face. Madonna had *such* a face. The nudes I've done are lovely. There's something wonderful in a beautiful form that happens to be somebody's body. One of my roles is to make people look at nudes differently. I'm trying to make people feel less uptight about their bodies because we're living in a puritanical age.

He said that his students had to pay cash to Madonna for modeling. She couldn't take checks because she didn't have a bank account.

Photographer Lee Friedlander, who was awarded a Medal of Paris in 1981 and has been awarded three Guggenheim fellowships, says of model Madonna: "I was curious to try my hand at the nude. She seemed a very confident and streetwise girl. She told me she was putting a band together, but half the kids that age are doing that. She was a good professional model."

The Friedlander and Schreiber photographs reveal Madonna still in her European mood. Her armpits are unshaven. Her hair is dark and curled. In some pictures she's pouting, in others she looks pensive. In one she stares warily at the camera. As well as she might have. After she became a pop sensation, her naked body was all over the pages of *Playboy* and *Penthouse* magazines. The black and white nudes of the ten-dollars-an-hour (sometimes cut rate to seven-dollars-an-hour) model sold for more than $100,000 to *Playboy*. And Schreiber and Friedlander revealed that their picture sessions with Madonna, which were published in *Playboy* in 1985, were a "job lot." They had paid her only twenty-five dollars for her time.

Madonna did a little better from photographer Bill Stone, who sold his pictures—he will not say for how much—to *Penthouse* magazine. "I was going to write her a check, but she wanted cash," recalls Stone. "I fished in my pockets for all the money I had and it was fifty dollars. She said, 'I can't take that much money.' As she was leaving she said, 'I can't take all of your money—take some back.' And she handed me a few dollars."

Others were also able to cash in on Madonna's modeling days. Madonna had attracted many people during her months in New York. One was Stephen Lewicki, who persuaded the nineteen-year-old to appear in *A Certain Sacrifice*, a soft-porn exercise which is guilty of being both exploitative and boring. You have to think if Madonna had made a porno movie, it would at least not be boring. In *Sacrifice* she's involved in a rape scene in a coffee shop, an orgiastic dance session, and a ritual sacrifice. *High Society* magazine paid out $100,000 for outtake nudes of Madonna from the film. She had been paid a total of one hundred dollars to appear in the movie. (Madonna later sued Lewicki to stop him using her name when he released the film—Madonna nude suddenly made this dull exploitation film a marketing possibility in 1985).

Madonna brazened out the nude pictures when they surfaced. But they did get to her:

> At first, the *Playboy* pictures were hurtful to me and I wasn't sure how I felt about them. Now I look back at them and feel silly that I ever got upset, but I did want to keep some things private. It's like when you're a little girl at school and some nun comes and lifts up your dress in front of everybody and you get really embarrassed; it's not a real terrible thing in the end but you're not ready for it. It seems so awful and you seem so exposed. It's other people's problem if they turn them into something smutty. That was never my intention.

Back in 1980 Madonna's dream of stardom was still just that. It was time for Little Orphan Annie to meet Mae West. Another example, as Mae undoubtedly would have observed, of goodness having nothing to do with it. It was literally the time for flash/trash. Madonna's desperation showed in her choice of outfits—she was hanging out in New York bars wearing little more than her underwear. She craved attention. There are the tales of her scholarship with the famed Alvin Ailey American Dance Theatre, but they are just stories. She was asked to work with the Theatre's third company, which is much like being in the reserves.

What Madonna had quickly found out was that she wasn't the only ambitious girl in New York. It was like being in the movie *Fame*—everyone could sing and dance and wanted a break. The Madonna of the University of Michigan, spiking her hair, tearing her leotards, and being different, lasted for thirteen weeks. She went to train with Pearl Lang, who was a protégé of dance legend Martha Graham. Madonna's father came to visit. Her apartment at 232 East Fourth Street was cockroach city. Silvio Ciccone pleaded. His daughter told him fame and fortune were just around the corner. Madonna left the legendary teacher because of what Madonna called "a lot of pain and angst."

At this time she also ended an affair with an artist she'd been seeing. Friends say he broke up with Madonna because she was not "inventive" enough sexually.

Madonna continued to take dance classes. She was also partying—and at a party she met Dan Gilroy. Gilroy was here, there, and also renting an abandoned synagogue in Corona, Queens. He and his brother Ed lived and rehearsed there. They were musicians. They were also Madonna's passport out of the cockroach gulch.

Gilroy says:

> She never really liked modeling. She would come home and complain about it sometimes or she would talk about how some photographer had tried to come on to her. She posed for me, too. I did paintings and sketches, but she didn't like staying in position so I'd let her read and relax when I was painting. She made better money modeling than at any other job she could get.
>
> Madonna was beautiful and alive and wanted to be a star. She'd wake up every morning, grab a quick cup of coffee, and get right on the phone calling her contacts, getting her career moving. She'd call anywhere and everyone. She worked hard. She learned to play drums with us. She'd practice five hours a day. She was a dancer and she had a sense of the beat. We got to be very close. We were sleeping in the basement of the synagogue and using its large meeting room as a rehearsal

and recording studio. My brother Ed and a beautiful blond girl named Angie Smit were also in the band. We were pretty good, but the gigs just weren't there. We might get one or two paying jobs a month and if you got eighty dollars a night, that was a lot. And we were dividing the money four ways.

She modeled once or twice a week. Sometimes she enjoyed the sessions if the photographer or artist was very good and professional. Once she gave me some beautiful nude photos that she was very proud of. She even wrote a little Chinese poem on a card attached to the pictures. It talked about how some people want women to have bound feet, but others want women whose feet are free. Maybe it was her way of saying she was free and liberated.

Madonna would go to the corner market and bargain with the countermen for the best vegetables and fruit she could get for the money. One time we were on hands and knees looking for loose change to buy a few potatoes. We had fun, too. We'd go dancing, but only on weeknights when it wasn't too crowded and we could really move around the floor. Our only luxuries were bicycles. Madonna was young. She was influenced by the people around her. When we played our gigs, Angie dressed really sexy with see-through clothes and she moved sensuously on stage. And Madonna began to do these things too. She was dark-haired then, but she saw Angie's long blond hair got the attention when she was on stage. Maybe that contributed to her finally going blond.

Gilroy and Madonna and the band they called the Breakfast Club stayed together for a little more than a year. If things had gone differently when she got a chance to perform in Europe it might have been more a matter of days. Madonna has always taken every opportunity. Back then, she had little thought about anything but advancement.

Patrick Hernandez was a discotheque pinup, all movement and not too much substance. He had success with some disco drivel titled "Born to Be Alive." Madonna was offered a job dancing and singing backup for him. In Paris. Paris, France, that is.

Madonna was on Cloud Nine. Seventh Heaven. She squeaked her delight to anyone who would listen. Michigan to Manhattan. And now, April in Paris? *D'accord, cherie.*

5

April in Paris

All I wanted to do was make trouble because they stuck me in an environment that didn't allow me to be free.—Madonna in 1984

The Eiffel Tower. The Champs Élysées. The city where a young girl's thoughts turn to . . . misery and loneliness. In Paris Madonna had an apartment, a maid, and a voice coach. Producers Jean Claude Pellerin and Jean Van Lieu, the Two Jeans, said they would make her the new Edith Piaf. Like so many before her, Madonna was to hear those immortal words: "We want to make you a star." It was a Pygmalion fantasy for the Frenchmen who had brought Hernandez's act to France. Now they could work on Madonna. But she was no fair lady. She wanted to work, to sing and dance, and not be touted around town as an upwardly mobile urchin. She'd picked up enough French to get the drift of the pitch from the Two Jeans.

Madonna reacted quite typically. She rebelled. If they wanted her to be at a certain restaurant she'd be out and about with a Vietnamese boyfriend who had an enormous asset—a motorcycle for scooting through the Paris traffic.

When she went on tour with Hernandez to Tunisia she was more enthusiastic about the nightclubs than his act. During the tour she went swimming. In a one-piece body stocking. She stuck out on the beach.

Back in Paris she'd order a string of desserts in very proper restaurants just to embarrass her hosts. This was not the France of Bardot and the films Madonna had seen in Rochester. She was all but dismissed and no one talked to her in English.

She was annoyed and upset to the degree her personality dictated—mad as hell.

Madonna was just an ornament, not the star ornament, not the star of this particular road show. And she didn't like it. The Two Jeans gave her money to keep her quiet. They introduced her to French boys. She liked French boys; their trim hips and interest in fashion. The more effeminate the men she met were, the more intrigued she was. She feels the same today: "I see them as my alter egos. I feel very drawn to them. I think like a guy but I'm feminine. I relate to feminine men. When I was in the ballet world, I wished I was a boy because I just wanted *somebody* to ask me out. Actually it would be great to be both sexes."

Jean Claude Pellerin's wife Michelle recalls Madonna's impact on the men of Paris, both the potbellied and the slim-hipped: "She stayed with me and my husband in Paris. She was very beautiful and she dated a lot of French boys. She thought they were very old-fashioned and she was very free. Very free and very liberal. She wanted a lot of boys. She liked the attention.

"But she *really* only wanted to be one thing—to be a star. And when she left Paris, she promised me she would come back as a star."

Of course, Madonna kept the promise. She returned a star, but in her individual way, as always. She distracted the catwalk models at 1990's spring fashion shows by wandering around in short skirts that often revealed she was wearing no underwear.

Madonna spent five indulged months in Paris. However, her French mentors had flopped at their attempt to pull off a Professor Higgins act. It was that young man back in Queens, New York, in the rented synagogue, who was to provide the initial spark for the Madonna magic. Dan Gilroy had kept up a steady stream of letters to Madonna. "We miss you. You must return to America." She did, driven back by frustration, and a debilitating attack of pneumonia. She called the synagogue from Kennedy Airport. She was back on stage with the Breakfast Club.

Madonna and the Gilroy brothers and Angie Smit made music and love together. It was a freewheeling time and Madonna felt the happiest she had ever been in her life. She felt loved. She felt wanted. And needed. She was writing songs now and not just playing the drums, but any instrument that Dan or Ed Gilroy would help her with. Madonna had the business brain. She was also the "balls" of the group as the others recall it. *She* went about trying to set up appearances, record deals: "I think I was just naturally more charming to those horny old businessmen than Dan and Ed Gilroy."

From her earliest days with Daddy, Madonna had known how to twist men to her point of view.

And there was always her *fear*. A morbid fear of death ever since her mother died. Madonna has already lived longer than her mother. What about Marilyn? She died at thirty-six. Madonna thinks about that now. But despite her fear of death, there was no hesitation in jetting in from Michigan, suburban street-smart but still Manhattan naïve: she was a ripe, well-built cherry parachuting blindly into Times Square, the Big Apple's rotten core of pornography and drugs and prostitution. There was no fear in going to Paris and literally living off the kindness of strangers. Or running with the Vietnamese and Algerian street gangs.

But deep inside herself there was an irrational fear. Of failure. Of being alone. Of dying. Most of us share some of these fears but most of us also tend to shove on through them and get on with living. Madonna fed off her fear. It was the catalyst for her unique and exceptional career which was about to explode like a fireworks display. There were some flying sparks to deal with first. She wasn't fearful about them.

The Gilroys had been trying to make it for five years. They knew their music. Madonna's motto was: "What do you know? Teach it to me." She was pushing, and pushing hard, and later it would sound harsh when she talked about those particular early days: "I took advantage of the situation. I wanted to know everything they knew because I could make it work for my benefit."

Gilroy found himself something of a Dr. Frankenstein. He'd created a problem. Madonna wanted to sing in the band, the band already had a singer. He was torn between his loyalty to his brother Ed and to Madonna, who also wanted to sing her own songs. She had turned into a monster for Dan Gilroy.

"She was fun, you know. But I knew that with that kind of drive and devotion to getting ahead something had to happen. I don't know if she was more talented than the rest of the group. More driven, and an incredible attention-getter. It was fun. It was a good year."

The romance, the learning, and her role with the Breakfast Club were over. Madonna left the synagogue. Queens was dead. Long live the big city.

Back in Manhattan, she called on the contacts she had established. She rapped her knuckles on record company doors. There were new boyfriends, one for Sunday, Monday, Tuesday, and so on, and—if she didn't get confused—it would all work out on Saturday night. One man she invited to a party asked if he could bring a date and was told: "Sure, bring a date. We can *all* do something."

But Camille Barbone still says all the boyfriends didn't mean a roundabout of sex. It was contacts. "She called herself a Boy Toy, but in no way was she a career prostitute. She didn't have to be. Madonna is a sexual creature who has men eating out of her hands. She knows about timing. A simple word like 'Hi' delivered by Madonna and men are reduced to stuttering and stammering. She had men lending her money and musicians rehearsing and giving their time without pay—and she wasn't sleeping with any of them."

She was sleeping in New York's garment center in a twelve-story structure called the Music Building simply because it had been converted into a series of rehearsal rooms. Madonna was still scrounging food on the streets—and accommodations in the building. When the last group left the place, she snuggled down for the night. In the morning, before the first group arrived, she'd use the basic toilet facilities.

Madonna took pride in making do. People couldn't understand how she lived. The popcorn. The daily apple. The bought meal. The borrowed five bucks. She was feeding on fear. And she was ravenous.

Around the New York clubs, she was known as a bit of a "cock teaser," a pragmatic one. After she got things—shall we say, "stimulated"?—she got her way, but those stimulated did not necessarily get theirs. But for most men it didn't matter. It was a turn-on, a thrill. She was funny. Rude. Terrific to look at. Sexy. Fun to be with. She was an all-around entertainer. A dangerous and different one. Because you never knew what you were going to get. It's the same today. She frightens. She fascinates. Back in New York, she was more interested in being fascinating. Again, fate blessed her. Steve Bray, the tall, pony-tailed waiter from the Blue Frogge in Detroit called. She needed a drummer. He was in New York in six days. He brought some musical know-how and "cool" to the motley band Madonna had gathered around her.

Bray moved in with her in the Music Building. He sensed Madonna was not held in the greatest awe by the crowd who used the rehearsal halls. "I think there was a lot of resentment of someone who has obviously got that special something. There are so many musicians out there, but there are only a few who really have that charisma. That community frowned on her. She had trouble making friends."

It was like a commune. Madonna wasn't a commune person. She was a Madonna person. A solo act. She wanted to call the group "Madonna." The self-effacing Bray told her that was an upsetting idea. Madonna belted out songs. "The problem," says Bray, "was that she seemed to attract all the really rotten guitar players in New York." They called themselves the Millionaires, and then Modern Dance, and then Emmy (a nickname Dan Gilroy had given Madonna). Madonna made a demo tape. Camille Barbone heard it. She was managing rock bands around the city at the time. A deal was done. For the first time in her life, Madonna was on salary. She knew how to spend. "Outttaaahere!" was the cry. The Music Building was history. She moved to New York's Upper West Side. Steve Bray moved uptown too.

The new band was called "Madonna." Camille Barbone had been promised old fashioned rock 'n' roll. Madonna wanted funk, funk, and funkier. There were shouting matches. Madonna went with rock 'n' roll but she was, as always, influenced by those closest to her. They wanted to be cool. Even cooler. All day she would write the songs with Steve Bray that the two of them wanted, but at night at the clubs they'd play the music the management— both their own and the clubs'—wanted.

They'd play the Roxy. Or the Danceteria. Which was where Mark Kamins changed Madonna's life. Well-connected, in many senses, Kamins was a disc jockey who mattered. And his Saturday night crowd liked to impress him. At Danceteria, Kamins was a star and he had his groupies. He came on to Madonna. She flirted right back. She got what she wanted.

Kamins listened to the demonstration recording made by Madonna and Steve Bray which included a song called "Everybody." Kamins adored it. It became one of the specials at Danceteria. The kids danced to it—they had to. Kamins recalls: "Everybody going to nightclubs has other ambitions, but she was special."

So special that Kamins helped finance a re-recording of that demonstration tape. And negotiated—solo—a deal for her with Sire Records. It was a *big* rung on the ladder.

Steve Bray was beside himself. *He* would produce Madonna's first album. Kamins was hopelessly happy. *He* would produce Madonna's first record. Wrong. Both of them. Madonna was scared. She felt she had been handed a golden egg—and she wanted it hatched by experts.

The Experts

Even when I was a little girl, I knew I wanted the whole world to know who I was, to love me, and be affected by me.—Madonna in 1985

The challenge of channeling Madonna's enormous, but often erratic, energy into her first album went to Reggie Lucas, who had previously produced for Stephanie Mills and Roberta Flack. It happened in a roundabout way after Madonna had put herself in a position of being worth hundreds of thousands of dollars. And it followed much Madonna-manipulation behind the scenes. Both Mark Kamins and Steve Bray had their hopes, but Madonna had her own dreams and also her own way of pursuing them at the Danceteria, the four-storied Chelsea discotheque that offered funky music and hospitality to a crowd that favored skin-tight leather, purple hair, and anything exotic, and *different*. Mark Kamins had contacted Michael Rosenblatt, a music world talent scout who worked for Sire Records, the "New Wave" arm of the giant Warner Brothers Communication Group.

Rosenblatt caught what amounted to performances by Madonna

47

at the Danceteria. These were the days of the belly-button look. Madonna wore jangles of jewelry (she got it free from Maripol, a French designer who was on the scene), and every piece of clothing had a suggestive rip or tear. Some of the Danceteria crowd say that at times Madonna looked as though she'd been through a spin dryer. Madonna also wore her "Boy Toy" belt. Not everyone got the humor. When she was living in the East Village, Madonna's hangout was the Roxy. It was full of graffiti artists and break dancers. All of them had nicknames which they would write on the club walls. There would be "Hi-Fi" or "Whiz-Kid." The game was to see how many times you could get this tag name up on the wall. The slang was you "threw up" your name on the walls. Madonna threw up her Boy Toy. The crowd thought it was hilarious. Madonna saw it as a tongue-in-cheek statement, the opposite of what was meant. She was not available to anyone—but outside of the Roxy no one knew that. The controversy was beginning, the slut label that had haunted her school days was back again. Madonna resents that. And the talk that she slept her way to success. Sure, she learned music from a string of guys, some of whom she had sex with. It's not that she is annoyed at the suggestion she used sex to get where she wanted—just furious that anyone thinks *Madonna* couldn't get there simply on her own talent and drive. That is what is insulting.

Also bothering her then was her almost-two-year relationship with Kenny Compton, who was a club-scene sexual Sir Galahad: he'd help any maiden he met. Madonna never slept with anyone else during her time with Compton. He did. Often. And it was the sexual promiscuity of some of her partners rather than her own which later convinced her to take a test for AIDS. The result was negative.

Such scary thoughts were not in the atmosphere of the Danceteria when Madonna's ambition and plotting were about to get her the result she so desperately wanted. When Michael Rosenblatt saw her at the Danceteria, he scented "a find" and a big-dollar one at that. He remembers that when he first saw Madonna at the disco club he thought two things: she looked wild and she looked beautiful. On stage she danced to Kamins's re-recording of her "Everybody." A deal was about to go down.

Seymour Stein was in Lenox Hill Hospital suffering from heart problems. As the boss of Sire Records, he had to finalize any recording deal with Madonna. A stocky man with what hair he has left worn in tight, gray curls, Stein is a music mogul. He got to the top spotting talent and trends. The buzz on Madonna was so strong that he agreed to meet her in his hospital room. He shaved, combed his hair, and got a new dressing gown for the meeting. The nurses told him not to get so excited, to watch the stress. By the time Madonna arrived, he had forgotten all about his dressing gown. He had a drip feed in his left arm and was sitting by his bed wearing his underpants.

It was a strange, but, with hindsight, totally appropriate beginning for the Material Girl's career. Stein, although impressed by Madonna's tape which he had played on one of the giant "portable" stereos in his hospital room, was still the wily businessman. He committed—but just so much. Madonna would be paid five thousand dollars as an advance for a contract to make three singles.

It was Easter 1982 when she went into a recording studio to make "Everybody." The record was showcased at the Danceteria—and what a showcase. She got three dancers—one of them was gay artist Martin Burgoyne with whom she had roomed before the Breakfast Club—and they put on a sensational act. It was raunchy. It was sexy. It was sensational. It blazed out dollar signs. In neon. Seymour Stein was there to watch her. So were Steve Bray and Mark Kamins.

Fans said she sounded "black." She was not pictured on her record covers. It was only when she appeared in public that they realized this five-foot-four-inch Italian-American was the one pounding the sound out. The irony of these appearances was that she was asked to lip-sync to her record and was getting paid more than when she had performed properly. She was being heard in gay clubs, black clubs, transvestite bars, rock clubs, every place they were making music. Her next record "Burning Up"—again a twelve-inch disco single—came out with a cheaply made video. In it, Kenny Compton appeared as a driver who was trying to run over Madonna. In reality he mowed her down. He told her their romance, which had really been an on-off, very sexually motivated affair, was off. Permanently.

Madonna moped for some moments then bounced back. She

likes smooth skin, lips, and the Latin look in her men. Enter John Benitez, aka "Jellybean" Benitez. "She didn't bowl me over at first. Then we started holding hands and buying each other little presents." They became a solid item—she even took him home to Rochester. Her father approved of Jellybean more than the outlandish all-black outfit his daughter wore for Thanksgiving Dinner. Now a respected producer, Jellybean was then the resident disc jockey at the Funland Discotheque in New York. Now he makes his own music. He and Madonna have remained very close. Interestingly, he says their first couple of years together were glued by mutual ambition: "We both started to move at the same pace. We're both very career oriented, very goal oriented. We both wanted to be stars." And Madonna never more so than when Sire Records told her it was prepared to bankroll an album.

She turned her back on Bray and Kamins. It was a bitter falling out with Bray, who told Madonna she had no ethics. "It was very hard to accept," he says. But he had no choice. He joined Dan Gilroy and the Breakfast Club, another crowd Madonna had left behind. Kamins was in the same position.

"Sure, I was hurt," he says. "At the time, I felt stepped on. But I don't think there's a mean bone in her body. Maybe a knuckle, but not a mean bone."

Maybe not mean, but tough. "All my boyfriends turned out to be helpful to my career. That's not the reason I stayed with them. I loved them all very much. I'm not Alexis from 'Dynasty.' All the men I stepped over to get to the top—all of them would have me back because they all still love me and I love them."

Professionally, the man who really mattered at that moment was record producer Reggie Lucas. He didn't last long. The album *Madonna* was released in America in July 1983. The first single from it was "Holiday," a song which had been brought to her by Jellybean. Everyone had enormous hopes for it, but it made only a minor splash. Later, there were radio plays of "Borderline" and "Lucky Star." They were on the record charts, but not huge hits.

What was to make Madonna a star was her first video; quickly followed by a second. The videos were her breakthrough. Madonna's dance background, her sense of the outrageous, and her songs all blended together for the MTV generation. She just knew how to "come across" sexually, and later explained: "I've been in touch with that aspect of my personality since I was five."

Madonna had given Reggie Lucas the go-ahead for the "sound" of her debut album but she didn't go for the finished product. It wasn't her. Too sharp, too sleek, too impersonal. She felt she was as good a judge as the professional producers. And she told them so.

"I wanted to push her in a pop direction," recalls Lucas. "She was a little more oriented toward the disco thing, but I thought she had appeal to the general market. It's funny about the thing with Kamins and Bray. The same thing that happened to them pretty much happened to me on her second record when they had Nile Rodgers." Lucas was dropped from the Madonna express. Madonna went after Rodgers who had worked with David Bowie and Duran Duran for her *Like a Virgin* album. Madonna was on the move—literally. In 1983 she had gone to London to promote "Everybody" and appeared at the Camden Palace club where a couple of years earlier she had met the then top-of-the-pops Boy George. Madonna didn't even believe he had a group. All she remembered was he wore high heels and was surrounded by men dressed just like him. She was intrigued. She liked everything feminine. But she wasn't in control of this particular adrogony and she didn't hang around to watch the action.

Even a dozen months after the release of her first album, which was dedicated to Silvio Ciccone, Madonna was not really a "name" outside of the New York club circuit. She could go to the Danceteria—a class-of-'82-type reunion—and not be mobbed. Or throw-up with the boys at the Roxy. It was no preparation for the giddy world she was joining. She was quick to realize this and sought out expert help. Her antennae yet again twitched at the right time.

Nile Rodgers introduced Madonna to the idol of her Detroit days—Diana Ross. She met Barbra Streisand. She was moving in the legend league. She wanted someone to guide her to that sort of status.

"Who's the best manager in the world?" she asked Rodgers and Jellybean Benitez. She didn't wait for their answers. She thought it out herself. Who was the biggest pop star? Michael Jackson—go to the top of the class. No, go to California and meet Jackson's manager, Freddy DeMann.

DeMann is always dapper, his moustache neatly trimmed and his hair slicked back. He no longer works with Jackson. He works with Madonna. She appeared in his Sunset Strip offices on a hot, smoggy day in July 1983, around the time her *Madonna* album was in the record stores. She was seriously blond at the time. And determined. "She had that special magic that very few stars have," he remembers. DeMann was interested enough to fly to Manhattan to see Madonna do her stuff at Studio 54, then the hangout of choice for Bianca Jagger, Halston, the Andy Warhol crowd, and other upmarket trendies. That crowd didn't worry Madonna. DeMann was her concern. He had told her that he didn't rate Prince. She knew how exciting Michael Jackson was as a live performer. Would DeMann like her? Would he manage her? Yes. And yes again. A formidable partnership was struck.

DeMann was taking care of business. Nile Rodgers, who had crafted David Bowie's hit "Let's Dance," was in the recording studio with her, and so was Steve Bray, her friend from the crazy days of the Blue Frogge in Detroit and the squabbling days in New York. Bray and Madonna were writing together again and four of their songs went on the *Like a Virgin* album.

The fireworks were about to go off. The title track of her second LP was also the first single, and the video for it was filmed in Italy, against the backdrop of the pillars and marble of Venice. It was almost the end of Madonna's career, and for the banshees of a certain taste it's a pity that the lion didn't eat her. The lion? Yes, the tame lion who costarred with her. Just wasn't so tame, it seems. Madonna was to be performing confidently while the lion wandered over to her right side. She was not to be alarmed by it. She was provocatively leaning against a pillar—"You make me feel," hip push, "like a virgin," roll of the belly—when nudge, nudge, there's Leo the lion with his head between her legs. Right there! She says now that she was convinced he was going to take a bite out of her. She looked down from under her veil, looked away and then looked down again. Leo gave her the eye and then a deafening roar. MADONNA TURNS ON KING OF THE JUNGLE—how the newspapers would have loved that one.

Madonna was hot. The crucifixes, the bare midriff, the Boy Toy innuendo, and her blatant sexuality also made her controversial. The "Merry Widow" long-line bras she wore were not uplifting to the Moral Majority. And there were millions of angry parents having to cope with youngsters who just wanted "to be like Madonna."

Madonna and boyfriend, "Jelly-bean" Benitez, at the 12th Annual American Music Awards at the Shrine Auditorium in Los Angeles, January 28, 1985. (Paltrowitz/Galella, LTD.)

Madonna during rehearsal for a homecoming concert at Madison Square Garden, June 11, 1985. (Ron Galella)

Dancing the night away at the Palladium in New York City, June 11, 1985. (Anthony Savignano/Galella, LTD.)

After accepting the award for Favorite Female Video Artist at the 14th Annual American Music Awards at the Shrine Auditorium in Los Angeles, January 26, 1987. (Ron Galella)

On her way to a party following the premiere of *Who's That Girl* in Times Square, August 6, 1987. (Belfiglio/Galella, LTD.)

At the Hollywood premiere of *Truth or Dare,* flanked by film director Alek Keshishian (right) and brother Christopher Ciccone, May 8, 1991. (Albert Ortega/Galella, LTD.)

Attending a tribute to composer Andrew Lloyd-Webber at the Music Center, Los Angeles, February 25, 1991. (Albert Ortega/Galella, LTD.)

Strutting her stuff to a sold-out audience at the Sports Arena in Los Angeles during "Blonde Ambition" tour, May 11, 1990. (Smeal/ Galella, LTD.)

Madonna with backup singers Nicki Harris and Donna Delory at premiere party for *Truth or Dare*, at The Shelter, New York City, May 8, 1991. (Ron Galella)

Arriving at hotel with husband Sean Penn after AIDS Benefit at Madison Square Garden, July 13, 1987. (Smear/Galella, LTD.)

Madonna and Sean Penn on lunch break in Manhattan during rehearsal of David Rabe play *Goose & Tom-Tom*, August 13, 1986. (Anthony Savignano/Galella, LTD.)

Madonna with Rosanna Arquette during Pro-Peace Rally in Van Nuys, California, October 6, 1985. (Smeal/Galella, LTD.)

Leaving Sardi's after the 42nd Annual Tony Awards, New York City, June 5, 1988. (Ron Galella)

With *Dick Tracy* costar Warren Beatty after concert on "Blonde Ambition" tour, New York City, June 25, 1990. (Ron Galella)

Dr. Sam Janus is an associate professor of psychiatry at New York Medical College and author of *The Death of Innocence*. His analysis: "She was oblivious to the traditional standards of morality. The sexually explicit lyrics and her vulgar songs advocate prostitution." Oh, well. What does Dr. Danilo Ponce, a renowned professor of psychiatry at the University of Hawaii, have to say about that? "The whole image Madonna projects is that of a tramp—of a streetwalker eager to sell her favors to the highest bidder." Or her records? Dr. Ponce went on almost excitedly: "She flaunts her bare navel and dresses in lacy lingerie and black bras."

What an advertisement. The people at the legendary Frederick's of Hollywood, purveyors of all sorts of sexy underwear designed to give bottoms, busts, and ardor a boost, recall the height of the *Like a Virgin* controversy. As well they should. Their sales went way up. Especially the black Merry Widows. In the first six months of 1985, there was a 40 percent increase in sales, says John Chapman, the company's merchandise manager. "We knew her popularity was doing it. We were selling to a much younger element—girls were going for the innerwear-outerwear effect." Maidenform looked back at sales reports and found that their black push-up bra was a sellout. Lily of France said their all-over lace body briefer did "phenomenally" that year.

There were all sorts of ban-Madonna outcries. Margaret Scott, who is codirector of the United Parents Under God with headquarters in Belmont, California, was active in that outcry. Why?

"Our youngsters were being exploited and manipulated by Madonna. She took a public-be-damned attitude when it came to morals. Our kids were being victimized. The kids worshipped Madonna."

They called her "a porn queen at heart," "a corrupting Pied Piper," "a trashy tart," "a slut." The lady, they said, *was* a tramp. Madonna worried about that reaction for as long as it took her to unhook her bra. Her attention was on the Wannabes, the fans who were buying her records and sending her to the top of the charts worldwide. In America, around seventy-five thousand copies of "Like a Virgin" were dancing off the shelves daily. And the fans were desperate to see her live—she sold out three nights of concerts at Radio City Music Hall in New York in thirty-four minutes.

The old record of fifty-five minutes belonged to Elvis Costello and Phil Collins.

The Boy Toy was no longer to be toyed with. She says it was all her humor, the mocking and mixing of sex and virginity, of crucifix and crotch. She says the fans tuned in to her humor:

> For so long people had been telling girls: "You have to dress nondescript. You have to look masculine if you want to be in control." And here was someone being very sexy and having fun and dressing up and doing exactly what these little girls wanted to do. And making all the decisions and having power and success. The people who adored me were the children who understood where I was coming from. The people who loathed me, didn't get it, and my success pissed them off. There's a lot of idiots in the world. It makes for more interesting magazines. Wouldn't you rather read about a slut than a plain-Jane wallflower? I know I would. Anyway, I think it would be kind of boring if everyone just loved me 100 percent.

But Madonna *would* love it. A poll of half a dozen American psychiatrists indicated she has an I-want-to-be-loved complex. And if you don't love her, or agree with her, or do what she wants, that is it. Be gone.

This is her vulnerable spot. She has trouble with the other viewpoint, which is understandable when you are the most recognized star in the world. But it doesn't help in personal or business relationships. Her two years of living with Jellybean in a New York loft were almost over. He also wanted to be a star and was producing and recording on his own. There wasn't room in Madonna's world for two stars in the family as she was soon to terrifyingly discover.

Madonna's goals were endless. Her records were all over the pop charts. She had six at one time in the American top forty. She was working on her body, determined to be the healthiest and fittest star.

She had played a cameo role as a nightclub chanteuse, warbling two of her own songs in Jon Peter's film *Visionquest*, and way inside her she still wanted to be a movie star—a star, a big, major, massive, incredible, adored legend like Marilyn Monroe.

The Movies

I can't conceive of living happily ever after or happiness for a long period of time with one person. I change so much and my needs change also.—Madonna in 1984

In the late summer days of 1984, Madonna spent a lot of time in her SoHo apartment in New York simply thinking, trying to clear her mind. She'd climbed on to the rainbow. Now she wanted to ride it. As fast as possible. She knew she would have to go on tour. But she also wanted the movies. And she'd heard about a picture that might just be for her. In one of the most amazing—if somewhat lucky—marketing coups in show-business history, her desires dovetailed. It was as if someone had waved a wand and granted her every wish.

Also living in a SoHo loft was filmmaker Susan Seidelman, who in 1984 was thirty-one, ambitious, and the director of the cult movie *Smithereens*, the surprise hit of the 1982 Cannes Film Festival. Seidelman sat on cushions to protect her spotless varnished floors while she read the script of a film titled *Desperately Seeking Susan*. It was something of a New Wave fairy tale with Susan dis-

rupting the everyday and sex lives of all involved. The film relies
on that elderly plot device, loss of memory, temporary amnesia. In
this case it is a New Jersey housewife named Roberta who loses
her memory and "becomes" Susan. Mistaken identities and farce.
Rosanna Arquette, who is like Audrey Hepburn masquerading as
Sophia Loren—with Arquette the gamin look meeting the full-fig-
ured woman—was offered, and accepted, the role of Roberta.

Susan was a small, five-million-dollar "budget" film for Orion
Pictures. To make it work, Seidelman needed a kooky, crazy, but
believable actress in the title role. She heard on the New York
grapevine—regarded as just ten minutes slower than the Hollywood buzz—that Madonna might be interested. Already 207 other
actresses had shown their interest and been tested. Madonna did a
screen test. Midge Sanford was one of the producers. Why did they
pick Madonna over all the others? "She had this presence you
couldn't get rid of. No matter how good the other people were, we
kept going back to her screen test."

Seidelman was all for Madonna. Orion Pictures executives had
never heard of the singer. As Seidelman says, and hard as it is to
believe now, Madonna was then "just a pretty pop singer." Ten
months later, she would have been out of reach for such a small
project. Then, she was prepared to work—and to learn. Her days
of being the wise guy, the comedian in the school playground
helped. So did the discipline from her dance training. "During the
nine weeks of filming, we'd often get home at eleven o'clock or
midnight and we'd have to be back on the set at 6:00 A.M. or 7:00
A.M. Half the time the driver would pick Madonna up at her health
club. She'd get up at 4:30 A.M. to work out first."

Madonna admits to "shitting bricks" when doing the early
scenes. But she was determined to learn. "I think I surprised everybody by being so calm—I was gonna soak everything up." She
admits that there was something of a self-caricature about her Susan. But only so far. "At first it was hard to get producers to take
me seriously because I was a rock star. I think they thought I would
throw fits or do blow [cocaine] on the set or something. I think
they were shocked when I showed up every morning like
clockwork."

As Madonna's fame increased, so did the interest in the film.
And Rosanna Arquette was disgruntled. A new song from Ma-

donna, "Into the Groove," was worked into the film. "The script changed when they got Madonna," said Arquette later. "I told them that if *Susan* was going to be a two-hour rock video, I didn't want to be part of it. A disco-dance movie wasn't what I signed on to do." And *American Film* magazine quoted her: "I don't think I'd ever want to be as famous as Madonna." Arquette denied that to me saying: "I never said that. But I think it might be a bit of a prison for her to have that kind of fame. I mean, she can't go anywhere and that's a lot to lose. I'm an actor and I want to be able to do different things. I'm not a megastar—that's a tough thing to be."

Madonna went to work on *Desperately Seeking Susan* in November 1984, and at the same time *Like a Virgin* was released. By the New Year, the album and the single would be sitting at the top of the American record charts. And Madonna's life was about to change irretrievably.

There were the business things: the fantastic success of the "Like a Virgin" tour which played to nearly 400,000 fans in twenty-seven cities with the Beastie Boys as the supporting band. On the last night of the tour, her father, Silvio, carried her off stage. The Material Girl was still Daddy's Girl. She renegotiated her record contract giving her much of the eight million dollars up front in a cash advance. She wasn't climbing the rainbow, she was sliding along it.

Personally, it was bumpy. Jellybean Benitez had sort of vanished with the New Year. "We were still friends. I know a lot of her ex-boyfriends and I don't think she used them or me. She took advantage of opportunities given her. Other people do the same thing," says Jellybean who, like most of her men, remains loyal. It was to get even bumpier that year. Madonna was to meet and marry Sean Penn, be rumored to be pregnant, have her naked body from her modeling days displayed all over *Penthouse* and *Playboy* magazines, and go to court to try and stop the rerelease of John Lewicki's soft-porn *A Certain Sacrifice*. Her lawsuit argued that it was a poor-quality film with an even poorer quality plot, never mind the orgies. Around that time, a ritzy apartment cooperative on New York's Central Park turned down her $1.8 million bid for a unit. They didn't want rock stars in the building. But Sean Penn wanted the Material Girl. Very badly. So badly that he played the romance without any of his trademark aggressive and impulsive style.

Opposites attract? They were similars. At least on the surface. Madonna was still fixated on Marilyn Monroe. Wasn't she the original Material Girl? For the "Material Girl" video, it was decided to reprise Monroe's best sequence from *Gentlemen Prefer Blondes*. Madonna would be Monroe. But she wanted to really get the feel of it. Bill Travilla, who designs for the ladies of the television series "Dallas" and "Knots Landing," was responsible for Monroe's shocking-pink cut-to-the-thigh gown in the 1953 film. He was surprised to see Madonna wearing it—or rather, a perfect replica of it—on her video. Travilla was not credited with the design but years later takes it in good humor, "I felt, to paraphrase Madonna, like a virgin. I'd been knocked off for the very first time."

The "Material Girl" video was also the first time Sean Penn got up close to Madonna. It was in a drafty recording studio in February of 1985. He, by no accident, turned up on the set of the video. He could hardly miss her fascination with Monroe. At this time, there was no evidence of Penn the hothead. They talked. They held hands. They did not date just each other and she said then:

> I didn't feel swept off my feet, but he is somebody whose work I had admired for a long time. He's wild, though. He'll probably die young. We have so much in common. We were born one day apart (Penn was born August 17, 1960) and he and I have similar temperaments. I feel like he is my brother or something. In fact, when I squint my eyes, he almost looks like my father when he was young. He's really smart and he knows a lot. He's willing to play the outsider or nerd rather than the hero that everybody likes.

Madonna and Sean Penn, the outsiders.

When they were first together on the West Coast, the doting Penn took Madonna on a forty-mile drive from his place in Malibu to Westwood, the university district of Los Angeles. At the back of the campus of the University of Los Angeles at California (UCLA) is Westwood Cemetery, the home of Marilyn Monroe's grave. Madonna was shaking during the visit. The ever-present rose from Joe

DiMaggio was on the grave. Later, Madonna said, "He really loved her."

And love, or an aberration of it, was to keep her going in the months ahead. No one—not even she or Sean Penn—knew what they were getting into. Madonna's early mentor, Camille Barbone, had something of an inkling when asked about that early relationship. She responded: "Madonna has always liked the rebel, the loner, in her men. James Dean is her idol. Ken Compton was a loner and so were her other lovers. Sean Penn is not the first rebel in her life and probably won't be the last."

Penn had been around show business all his life. His father, Leo, is an actor turned television producer and director, and his mother is onetime Broadway star Eileen Ryan. They doted on Sean and his brother Chris, younger by five years, and brought both of them up in the surf-washed, suntanned community of Santa Monica. The family later paid three million dollars to move up the Pacific Coast Highway and into a Malibu hillside home.

Penn was a schoolboy when he began working in local Los Angeles theater groups. At nineteen, he got a guest role on TV's "Barnaby Jones." There was more television work and then stage roles in New York. His big break came when he was cast with fellow Brat Pack member Tim Hutton in *Taps*. After that, he was a doped-out surfer in *Fast Times at Ridgemont High* with Phoebe Cates in her pre-black suspenders and *Lace* days. It was a sign of things to come when he "stayed in character" after the cameras stopped rolling. Director Amy Heckerling remembers he once "lost" his character but jumped right back into being surfer Jeff Spicoli by stubbing out a cigarette in his palm. *Bad Boys* director Richard Rosenthal is a Penn fan. That film stamped Penn's screen image. He played a teen gangster and grew his hair to his shoulders, ignored the makeup department for a real tattoo (a wolf's head), and only gave in on having his teeth filed down when his mother objected.

"He likes to get into character. He's the most talented actor of his generation," says Rosenthal who tells an interesting story:

We went out with some Chicago cops so Sean could get a "feel" of it all. During the raid, some more cops arrived and thought we were criminals and told us to raise our hands. I complied, but for Sean it was a chance to see what it's like for a gang member to take on a cop.

He turned to the cop, who was the size of an apartment, and said, "Fuck you."

The cop picked up Sean and threw him into a wall. His nose was almost broken, but later he told me it was at that moment he finally became his character in the film.

Less charitably, *Bad Boys* costar Reni Santoni recalls: "I thought the kid had been watching too many Brando movies."

Film executive Sherry Lansing who produced *Racing With the Moon*, which collapsed at the box office—Penn refused to promote the film in which he costarred with onetime lover Elizabeth McGovern—still believes Penn has got to do something about himself. "His career will be over if he doesn't change. He's talented but he's also self-destructive."

But for all his supposed publicity shyness, Penn eats out at places like Sunset Strip's Spago which is always a swarm of cameramen. Once he walked out of Spago and into friend and Brat Pack "godfather" Harry Dean Stanton. As flashbulbs popped, Penn zipped his jacket over his head and carried on the conversation with the bemused Stanton.

Penn liked proposing to actresses. First was Bruce Springsteen's sister Pam. He met the sister of the Boss during the filming of *Ridgemont High*. The wedding date was set for February 20, 1983. In April, a year later, he was set to marry Elizabeth McGovern. Madonna intervened.

Even Penn's father, Leo, shakes his head when quizzed about his older son's appeal for the ladies: "He has a big nose, small mouth, and close-set eyes. He's moody and likes mischief." And Penn himself tells a story which reflects just how far he is willing to go. It involves him and Brat Packer Emilio Estevez:

One time me and my buddy Emilio planned this thing. It was one of those times when we sat around and said, "We're really going to follow through on this. All the way. Nobody's gonna laugh."

This guy Kelly always got off the school bus with Emilio. So one day I was around the corner with another buddy in my car. We had .22 caliber machine guns with blanks. And Emilio had a blood squib—a big bag of fake blood. So he coaxed this guy Kelly into walking down to the ice-cream parlor with him.

We drive by—and open fire. Emilio does this great stuff. He squeezes the blood bag and it bursts all over his front. He hits the ground. Kelly has a skateboard in his hand, and he's freaking out. He starts to walk away in shock.

So we grab Kelly at gunpoint, put him in the back of the car, and we take off. He's so scared, he can't talk. We're wearing ski masks, and we're calling him Emilio as if we got the wrong guy, right? We go up into the canyon. We stop and tell him to get out of the car, and we say, "We're not going to hurt you, but we're gonna tie you to this tree and then we're gonna take off.

This was our greatest, ever: out of the back of the car we take this gasoline can—it's full of water—and my buddy lights a match. The guy starts screaming. I pour the water on the guy, and my buddy flips the match at him.

Then we tell him. Emilio arrives, and we have a little picnic. And the guy has never been the same since.

No one who meets Sean Penn ever is.

He says his mother told him long ago about dealing with executives: "She said when you go in don't picture them sitting behind a desk, but sitting on the toilet. It's amazing how that makes you strong." As long as you don't get flushed away.

Penn was enjoying strong reviews for *The Falcon and the Snowman* when he first met Madonna. In the film, he and Tim Hutton starred as the title characters, two young convicted spies. Penn identified with Andrew Lee Daulton, the real-life "Snowman" (he got the name for cocaine dealing) and still supports Daulton's efforts for parole. So much so that he overcame his shyness to appear nationwide television and say he would "do what I can as things come up. During the research for the role it was more than 'you scratch my back, I'll scratch yours.' I think it became a friendship and out of this, within the bounds of what a friend can do, I will. Under different circumstances, I'd like to sit down and have a beer with him. Maybe sometime we'll do that." But at a party for *The*

Falcon and the Snowman, Penn's shyness returned and he spent two hours huddled behind a potted plant.

You get the feeling that it would be uncomfortable if Penn were cast as Hitler because his "research" might involve starting a couple of wars. This deep research in changing mind and body is characteristic of Robert De Niro, but Penn insisted in a rule-breaking talkative moment: "The one thing I don't like to see written about me is the whole De Niro thing. I think it just doesn't matter. All that matters is what's on screen. I don't need to be thought of as a hard worker. I just want to be as good as I can."

"A lot of people will label him shy, but it's really just that he has a good sense of himself," says Oscar-winner Tim Hutton, adding: "He doesn't have to carry on or be an extrovert because he's got a real clear vision." It's a vision clouded by Garboesque and violent acts. He appears to believe rocks are mightier than the Penn and shows a touch of the primitive around the still camera—nervous, as though a camera click will kidnap his soul. One lady photographer at a publicity function with Penn confided: "He told me he had a water pistol and if I didn't leave he was going to fill the pistol with urine and squirt me."

When Sean Penn and I met, he looked more in need of a Bloody Mary than a shot of pee. It was 8:30 A.M. on Hollywood's Sunset Strip when they'd hosed the streets and they seemed to shimmer in the morning sun, clean after a night when they had been driven and prowled and mean. From three floors up in an art-deco hotel opposite the Comedy Store club, Penn, who is not known for laughs, was watching the traffic start to move. He started moving around the room. He has a powerful presence but looks more like a car hop with a hangover than a movie star. There's a lot of power in his right biceps as well as that tattoo of a wolf baring its fangs that he got for *Bad Boys.*

And we're there to do Madonna jokes? A couple of years earlier that would have appeared an exercise in something close to self-destruction, a different sort of angle on Madonna's favorite knock-knock joke routine. But by then, in 1988, Madonna and Sean Penn had been through marital mayhem and months of chaos, with the world media simmering or roasting them depending on the flavor of the month or the news of the day. Tits and ass sell—Madonna would more than likely make page one of any lively newspaper at any excuse.

That Saturday morning Penn was as precise as he would ever be about the two of them. He used the word "nigger" but carefully qualified that one had to understand how he was using "this vulgar expression." Go on.

> I think the problems came about because I wasn't a good little nigger actor who remained quiet, made films, and stayed out of the way of the press.
>
> Instead, I think I became labeled as the bad little nigger boy who married the white girl, a girl who was as white as they come. She belonged to them, to the public. And if anyone took her I think they thought it should be someone more acceptable like Donald Trump.
>
> The public is very possessive about rock stars and about her in particular. They don't want to share her love.

Neither, of course, did he. Madonna and Sean Penn were hormones in a hurry; fantastic passion, but then suspicious, and later paranoid, about their own and everyone else's motives.

But, in the beginning, everyone says it was true love. "I'd never known Sean happier," remembers his brother Chris. Charlie Sheen told me: "Sean's always been misunderstood. And probably most about how much he adores Madonna." Sheen's brother, Emilio Estevez, voted the same way: "I thought that was a lifetime partnership. I'd never write them off." Father Martin Sheen, the wise patriarch and honorary mayor of Malibu and misfits everywhere, said, "You just wanted it all to be perfect for them for they really were a well-suited couple. They both care and they both wanted to care for each other. I've often thought you can care too much and that spoils it."

"She could have had anyone she wanted," says Susan Seidelman who was part of the Madonna crowd at the time. "If it was just for the sake of getting married, she could have married someone richer, better looking, and more politically connected than Sean. I don't think she needed Sean in an opportunistic way. Movie people were already beating down her door."

For all the right reasons. She was becoming the hottest property in town. Any town. Anywhere. These were the Madonnamania days, the beginning: "Like a Virgin," "Material Girl," "Crazy for You," and "The Gambler" from the soundtrack *Visionquest* were everywhere. And suddenly so was *Desperately Seeking Susan.* Orion Pictures, which had been reluctant to hire Madonna, now wanted to promote her film. It opened in nearly one thousand theaters across America. It got a fair play from the critics. *Newsweek* said of the title star: "Not much subtlety is expected of Madonna or required—she has been typecast and fills the bill with delightful sluttishness."

Ah, a slut again. But being well paid for it. Madonna saw the humor. The reviews were mostly kind and called her "a new star." The clincher was that the film made money. And Hollywood, even if it had been ignoring Madonna's music, could relate to financial success. Madonna was hot. Hollywood was hot for her. From the Polo Lounge to Morton's, they were talking deals, packages, and marketing. Herbert Ross, the director who had made Streisand's *Funny Girl* wanted her to star in the story of stripper Blaze Starr (a project that would eventually get made with Paul Newman and newcomer Lolita Davidovich), and Ray Stark, who is still one of the most powerful men in Hollywood, wanted her to be involved in a project about 1920s torch singer Libby Holman. There was also talk of her starring for Disney in *Ruthless People* (Bette Midler got the role).

But her manager Freddy DeMann proved why he was what Madonna herself knew she needed. He caught the moment. Madonna was talking deals all over Hollywood. She was hanging out with Penn and the Brat Pack and even at the Hard Rock Café at the Beverly Center which was more of a tourist trap than a trendy hangout. There were also the clubs like Helena's with its incongruous location, diagonally opposite the tough Los Angeles Police Department's Rampart station where Robert Kennedy's assassin Sirhan Sirhan was held after the 1968 killing.

But Madonna was also working. She was back living out of a suitcase. Her concert tour took her to comparatively small stadiums. DeMann knew what he had. The fans wanted to see Madonna, as close as they could get. He knew it from the Michael Jackson experience. DeMann grins: "I wanted fans to be able to see her sweat." They saw her sweat first in Seattle. At the same time her Wazoo line of clothing—lace tops, skin-tight leggings, and midriff-baring uplifting underwear—went on sale. Maripol, her friend and jewelry designer who now has his own New York store, remembers those days:

"All the kids wanted to look like her. They were in the shop all the time. I called them the little Madonnas."

And variations of those little Madonnas turned out in hordes for every concert. The Wannabes ("We wanna be like Madonna") couldn't have cared less when old fogy Mick Jagger said Madonna's songs were pinpointed by "a certain dumbness." "Silly would-be pensioner," they thought. Madonna had been the hottest thing on Earth for at least three weeks, so screw the Rolling Stones.

It was hard for Madonna, even with all the entourage help and protection, to run herd on this overwhelming fame and acclaim. Her sister Paula said in a rare interview: "Everyone needs someone to hold on to."

For Madonna, it was Sean Penn.

They found a tryst of a place in the Hollywood Hills. It was a white building, like a castle in one of those fifties Hollywood epics when Errol Flynn was always the swashbuckling good guy and Basil Rathbone got skewered in the fading moment. For them it was romantic heaven. Was it haunted? For the practical of us, only by memories. The building had once belonged to legendary actor and boozer John Barrymore. That wasn't a good omen.

Romantics

I love being on stage and I love reaching out to people and I love the expressions in people's eyes and just the ecstasy and the thrill.—Madonna in 1985

Madonna's rags-to-riches-in-rags story was catching on everywhere. Her popularity grew with every play of her video on MTV, and she was on again and again and again. John Sykes was MTV's programming vice president when the Madonna phenomenon began: "Madonna is a prime example of an artist who could use MTV to launch a career. We had no negative feedback. What videos did was build up the expectations of her tour."

Madonna was preparing for her "Like a Virgin" tour by building a workout routine around a daily six-mile jog. Then, as today, she is almost totally vegetarian. She drinks Tab, chews sugarless bubble gum, and pigging out for her is cheddar-cheese flavored popcorn. The Boy Toy bad girl is always willing to be controversial, but also wants to be cholesterol free. She's a long way from bourbon swigging, drug-taking tragedies like Janis Joplin, Jimi Hendrix, and Jim

Morrison. Madonna may not be clean-cut on stage but her energy is.

In the weeks before she and Penn became exclusively attached and moved into the former Barrymore home, there was much action in both their lives. Madonna was on display. During her tour, the "Like a Virgin" number was designed to bring the house down—and did. She strutted on stage in a silk wedding dress with a twenty-four-foot-long train. This particular virgin bride would then crawl between the legs of her musicians. Attention? She got plenty of it. And the fans loved the subteen sexual humor. Madonna walked on stage with a stereo boom box and offered saucy jokes: "Every lady has a box. My box is special because it makes music—but is has to be turned on." Ouch! But her timing was perfect. Youngsters were looking for an outrageous performer, someone they could "adopt." And someone they could be like. They could wear the shirts, T-shirts, bracelets, and cross-shaped earrings that were on sale at every concert. The marketing men were delighted because they were selling faster than anyone could remember, faster even than fan paraphernalia at Michael Jackson or Prince concerts. You could see Madonna in concert, at the neighborhood cinema, on twenty-four-hour television, and on posters in kids' bedrooms in much of the West.

Sean Penn was being moody down in America's Deep South were he was making *At Close Range*. The film was being directed by his friend, and later best man, James Foley. They got on well and it was Penn who had persuaded Orion Pictures to give Foley the director's chair. Sean's mother, Eileen Ryan, was appearing in the film and so was his brother Chris. Christopher Walken was his costar in the murder mystery based on a real-life father-and-son crime syndicate.

Foley was one of the first to know how intensely the relationship between Madonna and Penn was developing. Others, mostly family members, soon found out. They were surprised. While Penn got stuck into the grind of making movies, the lady in his life was rivaling Princess Diana for newspaper and magazine space. She was supposedly dating many men, including Don Johnson, who was then on his roll with "Miami Vice." Dapper Don didn't make the cut, although he tried. She was a fan of Billy Idol, but for his music and naughty sense of humor, not his body. There were persistent tales of heavyweight trysts with John F. Kennedy, Jr., that offered gorgeous copy about Madonna following through on her Marilyn fantasy with a Kennedy. Some say it is a fantasy she has not totally dismissed. She met Prince during her concert tour and liked him for his hard work ethic, but was leery of him. Five-foot-three Prince turned up to see Madonna surrounded by bodyguards. She went along with her own bodyguards, one of whom reported that she announced: "Well, time to go visit the midget," which was no way to whisper sweet nothings.

The truth was that Madonna and Sean Penn were together every minute they could be. Although exhausted, she'd call him every night after her performance and they would talk for half an hour. She wound down. Penn would often be winding himself up, frustrated by his self-imposed chastity. He saw her perform in Miami and San Diego when he could get away from filming. And in Detroit, where he met her father and brothers and sisters. And found out to whom Madonna lost her virginity. School friend Carol Belanger remembers flipping though her high school yearbook with Madonna and Sean. They stopped at a picture of Russell Long— the Cadillac man. Belanger says she told Penn that Madonna "broke a lot of hearts." Penn was to turn around and do just that to the Madonna fans before the year was out. When the "Virgin" tour arrived in Los Angeles, the Penn family and members of the Brat Pack were there. The long, hot summer was not far off.

James Foley says he was respectful of Madonna's relationship with Penn. Of the premarriage days: "I'd known Sean for a long time and he'd never been happier."

Foley got lucky too. Madonna asked him to direct her new video for "Live to Tell" which was the closing song of *At Close Range*. He was glad to, but says, "Nobody knows what a major sweat those videos are."

Diane Keaton is a close friend of Foley's, and saw an early "cut" of *At Close Range* as did Madonna. They became a constructive critical group and Foley says: "Madonna is like Diane in that she has opinions and voices them without hesitation. Diane and Madonna have a lot of similarities and like and respect each other."

Sean Penn doesn't like or respect the press, particularly the suede-shoe variety from the tabloids of Britain and America. Lots of people don't. It's just that Sean's rather more exuberant about it.

In June 1985, the gossip factory was mass-producing stories that Madonna was pregnant. There had been hints that she and Penn were going to marry. Well, what other possible reason could there be for marriage? Love? Forget it—she a Boy Toy and he's a Wild Boy. Some of that thinking was correct.

A writer and a photographer from a British newspaper were sent to doorstep a motel on the outskirts of Nashville and get happy snaps of the "pregnant" Madonna who was visiting Penn on the *At Close Range* location. The lads got lucky or unlucky depending how you view it. They had no idea if Madonna would be there. It was part of the old journalistic tradition of when-in-doubt-send. They had been sent.

When Penn saw them, his face went bright red with rage. He hammered and punched the writer, threw a rock at the photographer, and then grabbed at his camera straps. Madonna was only a few steps away. She pulled a floral baseball cap over her eyes and ran back into the motel. A very nasty incident, which was not helped by the fact that photographer Laurence Cottrell had remained as cool as possible in the circumstances and kept his finger on the camera button. Photographs of the snarling Penn about to throw a rock went around the world.

The legend of the "Poison Penns" was building. And so was the talk of marriage. By now it was generally agreed they would marry—but when? And where?

The couple was hot. The new Burton and Taylor. They would star in a film titled *Pipeline* set in the Alaska oil fields. They would do the comedy *Blind Date* (Kim Basinger and Bruce Willis finally made that one), and every other producer in Hollywood trying to pitch a package was talking Madonna and Sean Penn.

On August 13, 1985, Madonna performed solo and with the Thompson Twins at Live Aid in Philadelphia. She was introduced by Bette Midler as "a woman who pulled herself up by her bra straps and has been known to let them down occasionally." Madonna had other thoughts as she strutted in Philadelphia. She and Penn were busy planning their marriage. Something old, something new, something borrowed, something blue? Try a more military strategy. Penn was to greet his wedding guests with: "Welcome to the remaking of *Apocalypse Now.*

He wasn't far off.

Madonna, who had boosted her career by being able to manipulate the public, wasn't such an artist when it came to privacy. She and Penn tried. The invitation, designed by Penn's brother Michael, read:

> Please Come to Sean and Madonna's Birthday Party on the Sixteenth of August Nineteen Eighty-Five. The Celebration Will Commence at Six O'Clock P.M. Please Be Prompt or You Will Miss Their Wedding Ceremony.
>
> The Need for Privacy and a Desire to Keep You Hanging Prevents the Los Angeles Location from Being Announced Until One Day Prior. RSVP by August 3 to: Clyde Is Hungry Productions, 6521 Leland Way, Hollywood, CA 90028, (213) 460-6208. *Please include a phone number where you can be reached.

Nuptials, Hollywood style. Don't call us—we'll call you. For all those guests hanging on for the wedding location there was time to buy a wedding present. Madonna had gone the traditional route and registered a list of gifts she would like with a store. The Michigan girl who had begun her career living out of trash cans in New York, was registered at Tiffany's and had selected two china patterns: Monet's Giverny which then sold for $260 a place setting and Coeur de Fleur from Tiffany's private stock, which in 1985 was $660 a setting.

It was just one indication of how far and fast Madonna had traveled. In shopping malls across America there were regular weekend Madonna look-alike contests. She had been photographed in Hawaii for a "Madonna—1986" calendar, and Barbra Streisand had taped her video "Emotions" clutching a handful of photographs of Madonna. Hollywood was still at Madonna's door and the budget this time was fifteen million dollars for *Street Smart*, a film in which she and Sting and Prince's protégé Vanity were to appear as a one-name rock trinity in a tale that sounded very much like *West Side Story*.

Madonna was out jogging in New York's Central Park when she first realized she could never again go anywhere in public without a bodyguard. Concentrating on her running for a time she didn't realize that she had been recognized. When she did look over her shoulder, she was being chased by about fifteen fans. She didn't know they were just chasing autographs and she panicked. She hurdled a fence and fell. She only scraped a knee, but she'd lost control for a moment and swore that would never happen again.

But she had little control over the imminent remake, as Penn had put it, of *Apocalypse Now* on a bluff in Malibu. Penn's twenty-fifth birthday was on August 17 and Madonna turned twenty-six the day before. It was to be quite a party for them both. Penn— although facing assault charges and a civil lawsuit for his bad-boy behavior in Tennessee—seemed to have mellowed. He and Madonna had been playing house, renting the former Barrymore home for thirteen hundred dollars a month. They could see the HOLLYWOOD sign from the bedroom window. Madonna recalls when he proposed: "I was jumping up and down on my bed performing one of my morning rituals and all of a sudden Sean gets this look in his eye and all of a sudden I knew what he was thinking. I said, 'Whatever you are thinking I'll say yes to.' That was his chance, so he popped it." She says they celebrated by going out to a 7-Eleven convenience store and buying a bag of jawbreakers. Not a traditional proposal or celebration, but wedding plans followed in an orderly fashion. First there was Madonna's wedding shower which was hosted by Nancy Huang, the girlfriend of Nile Rodgers. Nancy invited Madonna's friends to her Upper East Side apartment in Manhattan. Mariel Hemingway and Alannah Currie, from the Thompson Twins, was there. Oh, and six male friends of Madonna who dressed in drag by way of celebration. The gifts were lingerie, a push-button sequined phone, and an assortment of jewelry. Madonna had bought herself a forty-four-thousand-dollar midnight-blue Mercedes which was parked out in California where the celebrations continued a couple of days later in Hollywood with a "bachelorette" party at the Tropicana, a tacky mud-wrestling club in a run-down area. Madonna went in a disguise of dark glasses, no makeup, her hair pulled back from her face, and looked just like Madonna in dark glasses with no makeup. She cheered as big-busted lady wrestlers flailed about in the mud.

Sean Penn was also getting ready for marriage—with a stag party. Madonna had the lady mud wrestler, but her husband-to-be was entertained by Kitten, who bounced off the measuring tape at

42–24–36. The party was in a private room above the Roxy night-club on Hollywood's Sunset Strip. Penn's brother Chris, Tom Cruise, Robert Duvall, David Keith, Harry Dean Stanton, and Cameron Crowe, who wrote *Fast Times at Ridgemont High*, were among the guests. The drinks were free. Kitten remembered: "They were all pretty buzzed. Sean was feeling no pain. But he didn't fall on his face or anything. When he talked, he made sense. He's a very nice guy. He reminded me of a little boy, like he was eight years old and had got so many cookies he didn't know what to do with them." Kitten Natividad did her strip routine with Penn slapping his knee in delight. Harry Dean Stanton arrived late, and Kitten recalls: "Sean picked up my blouse and said, 'See what you missed.' Then he shoved his face right into me. I didn't mind. Sometimes I do, but it was Sean's night and he could have done whatever he wanted. That was about as wild as it got."

No one really knows who leaked the location of the nuptials. But by the morning of the wedding, everyone knew it was in Malibu. By the afternoon the location was pinpointed. Television stations and newspapers rented helicopters and they did appear suddenly out of the sky like that famous scene in *Apocalypse Now*. I remember driving up Pacific Coast Highway from Santa Monica to Malibu to report the wedding for a British newspaper. It was midafternoon Friday and the weekend traffic heading north to Santa Barbara and Carmel and other retreats was already building up. The all-news radio was babbling the headlines and at the top of the news was *The Wedding*. Some commentator suggested it was the oddest coupling since Marilyn Monroe had been turned on by the intellect of Arthur Miller, the couple who became known as the Hourglass and the Egghead. With a blazing red sun dipping down into the Pacific it seemed more beauty and the beast that day.

The world wanted sensation. They got media mania. And star paranoia. Who was out of order? The choppers buzzed the wedding of entertainment's most visible couple, the reigning king and queen of what seemed to be everyday's headlines. Crowds crushed around the estate. Madonna and Penn could have slipped off to Las Vegas and avoided such fuss. They didn't. They did it traditionally—with a Grand Prix of twists—on one of the most material pieces of real estate on earth. Malibu is where you flaunt it rather than hide it. This is where you can lie on the sand and stare at the stars and vice versa. Madonna forgot her outlaw-black lace and wore an antique-white gown, a low-cut number designed by Marlene Stewart, who costumed Madonna for her "Virgin" tour. It was, recalls Ms. Stewart, designed as a "fairy-tale kind of thing with sort of a baroque feeling. We wanted a fifties feeling, something Grace Kelly might have worn."

Well, we *are* talking rock royalty. The Queen of Pop added one twist to the traditional by giving the finger to a buzzing helicopter as her mother-in-law, Eileen Ryan, dabbed wedding-day tears from her eyes. The groom also stuck his head up the bride's dress. A new tradition? Maybe a Malibu one.

To set off her Cinderella gown, Madonna wore her hair in a French twist with a black bowler draped in cream-colored tulle on top of it. What looked like a beauty contestant's sash was draped across the dress, a silver and pink metallic net covered in encrusted jewels. She walked down the white-ribboned aisle set out at the eight-million-dollar estate in shoes decorated in pearls and gold embroidery. Silvio Ciccone was at her side, as the helicopters buzzed like annoying flies in the clear blue sky above, for the ten-minute ceremony in which the couple exchanged plain gold bands.

The groom wore a dark double-breasted $695 off-the-rack Gianni Versace linen suit. Since the bride and groom were Roman Catholics the Malibu clifftop where they took their vows had been blessed by a priest. White ribbons had fluttered on the bluffs all day, like an open invitation to the helicopters that chattered all over them. White seats and benches, in sectioned, serried ranks, enough to accommodate two hundred guests had been laid out two hours before the ceremony at the lavish home of film producer Kurt Unger. Unger, a neighbor of Johnny Carson, is a close friend of Penn's parents. The massive catering tent was Pepsodent-white like the bunting and ribbons covering the tennis courts. White lily pads floated in the swimming pool. But there was anger among the guests over the helicopters which delayed the ceremony. Producer James Day says: "Guests were hoping Sylvester Stallone would turn up and do a Rambo on the copters." He didn't.

Everyone attending went through what seemed like presidential security. Tom Cruise, David Keith, Andy Warhol, Christopher Walken, Martin Sheen, Diane Keaton, and Carrie Fisher were all formally dressed. Cher set off her not-so-traditional outfit with a spiky purple punk hairdo. "I thought this was a secret," complained Rosanna Arquette as she submitted to being frisked by security men in smart slacks and blue jackets which hid their two-way radios. Penn had also arranged for guards with infrared binoculars to "frisk" the perimeters of Unger's estate. An Italian photographer wearing camouflage gear and a blackened face, for all the world looking like an SAS man, had been caught and ejected from his hunter's hide in the shrubbery just before the 6:30 P.M. ceremony.

Judge John Merrick, who conducted the bizarre event, recalls that despite the choppers, he thought it was "dignified." "I was shouting but she was answering as loud as she could. I think she enjoyed it all."

"The ceremony was lovely. Madonna was lovely, but I couldn't hear a thing—nobody could," recalls Oscar-winner Christopher Walken. As the official ceremony ended, Vangelis's *Chariots of Fire* theme started up. Penn lifted the veil pinned to Madonna's black bowler hat and gave her a lingering kiss. Then, hand in hand, they clambered up to the balcony, and grinning, began waving to their guests. Madonna leaned backward to the crowd before hurling her bouquet of white roses into the sky. It was aimed toward a group of her single girlfriends. "Catch it, catch it," she yelled at them. The Bad Boy and the Boy Toy were wed and Penn toasted, "The most beautiful girl in the world."

It might not have happened. Only a few hours earlier, Penn had decided to take out some of the early whirlybirds that were scouting the Malibu coastline. Armed with a pistol which he had stuck into the belt around his black Levis, Penn spotted a helicopter coming in over the ocean from the west. He hid in the bushes near the pool and then jumped out and got off two shots. When Madonna shouted at him he told her: "I'm not trying to hit it—I'm trying to scare it away." One of the catering staff, who did not want to give his name, said: "I was near the kitchen window when I heard the shots and I saw Penn holding the gun. It looked like a .45 automatic." The Malibu Police Department has no record of a report of a shooting incident before or during Madonna's wedding.

Madonna was so angry about the incident that she had to be calmed down by her family. Best man James Foley smiled through two weeks' growth of beard for most of the ceremony, and Madonna's sister Paula, who was matron of honor, helped pacify the bride and groom. They told the couple to forget about the intrusion and concern themselves with their own lives—and it was with a brave face that Madonna turned to her father before taking her vows and said, "Bye, Dad." The music was "Moments of Love," but as the music was drowned out by the helicopters, Penn's face got redder and redder.

Service was quick for the two hundred guests after the wedding ceremony. Malcolm McClaren's "Madame Butterfly" blasted from loudspeakers as waiters scattered around pouring from hundred-dollar bottles of Cristal champagne. A feast was served by the chefs from Spago: a five-tier hazelnut cake with sugar flowers, lobster ravioli, rack of lamb, swordfish, and baked potatoes stuffed with sour cream and caviar. Wines included California's Acacia Pinot Noir. There were three fully-stocked eight-foot-long bars.

Cher remembers a wonderful moment. When it came to cutting the cake, Madonna turned to her much-married friend saying: "Hey, you've done this before. Do you just cut one piece or do you have to slice up the whole thing?"

Outside, the members of the press were still gathered. One man armed with a two-way radio was trying to talk to his airborne colleague: "Mad dog to mad dog one . . . do you copy?"

Inside the guests were gasping at the wedding presents, which had a room of their own. There was a 1912 antique silver tea service from British producer John Daly, who was responsible for *The Falcon and the Snowman.* An antique jukebox with two dozen of Madonna's favorite oldies—half of them Motown numbers—from Mo Ostin, of Warner Bros. Records. And there were several sets of Tiffany china. Disc jockey Terence Toy had got the dancing going with some big-band swing numbers but by eight o'clock was beginning to liven things up. He blasted out Motown dance numbers and then Madonna's own "Into the Groove."

Groove was what the couple planned to do on their four-day honeymoon at the Highlands Inn in Carmel, the seaside community quietly settled between Los Angeles and San Francisco, and known around the world because of the two-year tenure of Mayor Clint Eastwood. For $225 dollars a night, the Highlands Inn offered peace, quiet, and the privacy which Penn and Madonna needed. One room-service waiter told of the day he delivered to their suite: "I couldn't believe my eyes. They were both sitting in the bath together—and they had their clothes on. And the bath was full of water. They were not embarrassed about it, but I was."

The couple was in room 429 and registered as M. Ochs, a bit of wordplay on "Madonna Ochs" —a name chosen by Penn. The late Phil Ochs was a sixties protest folksinger who was overshadowed by Bob Dylan. He became a disillusioned, forgotten, and extremely difficult character: "Phil was an asshole long before it became fashionable," said Penn, who liked the idea. He had driven them north in his black Mercedes. Madonna was wearing a black sweatsuit. "She wore the same sweatsuit for three days," recalls a maid who also revealed: "They brought their own beer cans with them. They gave me one and we all held hands while we had a drink."

Madonna appeared to survive on room-service strawberries and cream and supplies of champagne, orange juice, and popcorn from the hotel's food shop. One night, they went out to dinner at the Hog's Breath Inn, which is owned by Clint Eastwood. It's a favorite eating place for Carmel locals, but also popular with tourists. By going there—and why did they?—any belief that their whereabouts could remain secret was gone. By morning, the fans, the press, and the paparazzi were heading for Carmel. The honeymoon was over.

Reality and the business of finding a family home took its place. They had been looking for a long time. Penn favored something in Malibu with a good number of acres. One of his crowd remembers asking him if he planned to fence off any property he might get, and was told by an unsmiling Penn: "A fence, nothing. We're going to have gun towers." Madonna hadn't seen any gun towers in Beverly Hills or Bel Air where she'd been looking. Her search almost led to an embarrassing run-in with another material girl, Nancy Reagan. Playwright Neil Simon had put his lavish Bel-Air home up for sale. First Lady Nancy was interested but dithering. She looked around twice. Then she brought friends over. Then she arrived at separate times with three different sets of decorators. The Simon asking price was $3.5 million. All of this was unknown to Madonna who was being shown property by a Beverly Hills real-estate agent. She fell for Simon's property instantly and offered a bid closer to the asking price than the one Nancy had made. Simon was stuck. He pleaded a change of circumstance and took the house off the market.

Madonna and Penn were headed for a $3.5 million estate shielded by the mountains that used to be roamed by the Chumash Indians. They created more barriers with a high, electrified wall fence. Penn wanted more security. Steel spikes were ordered placed along the tops of the walls. It was a sort of marital Fort Knox. Despite that, it was the scene of some of Madonna's happiest moments. And her most terrifying.

For the moment, they were newlyweds scouting shops in Los Angeles and New York for furniture and bric-a-brac for their home. But by October there were already rumors that the marriage was in a desperate way.

Another Day,
Another Brawl

His temperament is similar to mine. That doesn't always make for an ideal relationship, but I don't know what will happen.—Madonna in 1985

It was only a few weeks after the wedding that Madonna sought psychiatric help. Her friends urged her to persuade Penn to get professional help too. When Penn had turned extraordinarily violent, into a wild-eyed madman, during his attack on the two British journalists in Nashville, Madonna had been speechless. "Throughout the whole thing she never said a word to either of us," recalls Laurence Cottrell, the photographer at the scene adding: "She just stood there and watched us as he did his thing with the rock."

Now it seemed like another day, another brawl. Seven weeks after the wedding, Penn was spitting and swearing at photographers outside Wolfgang Puck's West Side celebrity hangout Chinois, in Santa Monica. Madonna was covered up with a coat and laughing: "Where are we? I can't see where I'm going." Penn didn't find any of it funny.

"A Certain Sacrifice" with a brunette Madonna went on sale in video stores in October 1985 just as Madonna and Penn were driving, running, or hiding from photographers in Los Angeles and Manhattan. Penn went to Nashville to face his assault charges. He was fined one hundred dollars and given a ninety-day suspended sentence. On his way back to Los Angeles, the actor spotted a photographer. His abuse made no sense: "I wish I had AIDS so I could shoot you. I wouldn't do it fast, but slow, from the toes up."

Madonna and matrimony seemed to be bringing out all the acrimony in Penn. Around the celebrity crowd hangouts in New York and Los Angeles, they were known as "S and M." They were also one of the best-known couples in the world. Madonna had convinced herself that acting was what she wanted more than anything. But she was still deeply in love with Penn and determined, as a good Catholic girl should be, to keep the marriage intact. She also had much respect for Penn as an actor, as a mentor.

This was the start of another obsession for her—to win the title role of *Evita*. She had quietly met with producer Robert Stigwood, and Penn was unaware how keen she was on the role. With him, she was talking a joint project. But then, as now, Madonna wanted movie stardom on the Marilyn Monroe scale. She saw *Evita* as the vehicle to provide that. Seymour Stein, who had launched her career, recalls:

> I knew from the moment she walked into my hospital room that she would be a star. She had the kind of self-assuredness that convinced me she was a very determined lady. I don't know about ruthless. When men are ambitious they're called ambitious; when women are ambitious they're called ruthless. There's no ego problem there. She's in a hurry. She's very, very serious about what she does.
>
> She know what she wants. Her talent has been obscured because of the fuss about everything else. But nobody tells her what to do.

It also seemed that way to Hollywood producer Julia Phillips who had been involved in major box office successes like *The Sting* and *Close Encounters of the Third Kind* before she dove into an abyss of drugs. Phillips had a meeting with Freddy DeMann at Morton's restaurant in Hollywood and was won over by him. "He was managing Madonna, the hottest female to come along since Barbra Streisand." In her controversial best-seller *You'll Never Eat Lunch in This Town Again*, which chops up many Hollywood notables, Phillips writes about "taking a meeting" with Madonna and Sean Penn whom she calls, "the Prince and Princess." She says her martini arrived at the same time as the couple.

> I am torn for a moment between saying hello, changing seats, and taking a long sip. I do all three without embarrassing myself. She is dyed platinum and dressed from head to toe in black leather. He is in jeans and leather jacket, what a surprise. He is a dim bulb in her supernova aura. She has the same amazing pale perfect skin that Barbra Streisand has. I have always imagined that Marilyn Monroe's skin was like that too. It is impossible not to think of Marilyn Monroe when you see Madonna even if you know that that's because she has designed herself so that you will think that way.

Phillips asked if they wanted drinks. Madonna ordered a Perrier. Penn looked at Phillips's martini and started to order a beer. Madonna squeezed his knee and he changed his mind. The film discussions really didn't go anywhere concrete. But Phillips and DeMann continued to talk, to meet. She was pushing a female version of *Carnal Knowledge*. In Phillips's working of the film, Madonna would play the sexual experimenter. Madonna was taken by the thought of the memorable Jack Nicholson role, and, in turn, gave DeMann permission to pursue the idea with Warner Bros. But there were complications because of a similar project.

Still, every studio in town wanted Madonna in something. In anything. And they were miffed when Handmade Films, in Hollywood terms an upstart company, run by former Beatle George Harrison, won her services. Handmade had done *The Life of Brian* and *A Private Function* and now had Madonna starring in the fifteen-million-dollar *Shanghai Surprise*. The hook had been her co-star, Sean Penn, who would play a down-at-the-heel adventurer to

Madonna's missionary in 1930s China. They were getting one million dollars each. As well as some surprising perks. The couple would have total script approval, which was a nerve considering Madonna's lack of film experience. And they would have a double bed with Japanese screens in their dressing room. Their involvement in publicity for the film could be "requested" not "demanded."

Publicity? They got more than they ever dreamed.

The film was to be shot in Macao, a magical name since the RKO Pictures days when Robert Mitchum starred in a movie by that title, wooing Jane Russell and being chased by William Bendix. A city of intrigue, gambling, and mystery, Macao was colonized by the Portuguese in 1557. Relations between them and their one billion neighbors next door in China have always been reasonable.

The reasonable people of Macao were about to encounter a rather unreasonable young man. Sean Penn was becoming more and more insecure by the day. His wife was the entertainment world's hottest new talent and he was increasingly being regarded as difficult and excess baggage. Was he worth the trouble?

The *Shanghai Surprise* film company set themselves up in the Oriental Hotel, a tower block of East meets West accommodations with wonderful service. The stars were assigned two bodyguards trained in martial arts. Security men would seal off the swimming pool when Madonna wanted a paddle. The couple put on disguises to go out to restaurants. It was Leonel Borrahlho's job to see through the disguises.

Borrahlho was sixty-one when the Penns arrived in Macao and was the correspondent on the island for the *Hong Kong Standard*. Mr. Borrahlho, now retired and living in Macao, was a man of propriety and dedication. He was asked to get photographs of this famous Hollywood couple. While others doorstepped the lobby of the Oriental Hotel, the enterprising Mr. Borrahlho found out which floor the Penns were staying on. He then found himself a hiding place on the eighteenth floor near their suite. Late one afternoon he got lucky and unlucky at the same time. He was in position as Madonna and Penn and their bodyguards emerged from the elevator. From behind the door of a "blind waiter" he and his camera popped.

Penn panicked. "Who let you in? What are you doing here? Can't you see my wife's trembling?" Mr. Borrahlho says he saw Penn's fist coming toward him but it was stopped short by one of the bodyguards. The noise, and the scuffling left everyone seeing events differently. Penn's bodyguard tried to grab the camera which was hung around the photographer's neck. Mr. Borrahlho remembers karate chops and kicks as his camera strap held and his neck was injured in the tug-of-war.

"I was only doing my job. I didn't expect this kind of 'Ugly American' behavior," says Mr. Borrahlho. Seemingly, Penn's reputation for never meeting a photographer he couldn't wait to punch hadn't gotten that far east. Now it had arrived with force and Penn was to be called many ugly things over the next few days as all manner of legal wrangling went on. Leonel Borrahlho used his platform in the *Hong Kong Standard* and his political clout in Macao to make things as difficult as possible for the filmmakers, and particularly for Penn.

Madonna was angry and frustrated by the Penn-inflicted circumstances. She had liked the script for the film, which was based on Tony Kendrick's novel *Faraday's Flowers* and saw it as a chance to create something like *The African Queen* with her and Penn as a modern-day Hepburn and Bogart. She enjoyed the "feel" and the dressing up in period clothes. She turned herself into a Jean Harlow style platinum blond as Gloria, a woman who runs away from the Depression in America to seek fulfillment in the Orient. Madonna wanted to be fulfilled as an actress. She wanted to prove she could act. Gloria, she felt, was a woman so different from her that she would have to give an Oscar-worthy performance to pull the character off. Gloria, unlike her, she thought, was not in touch with her emotions. But both she and her character had to contend with Penn.

George Harrison and his Handmade Films also had to contend with Penn. Chris Nixon was the publicity man on the film. It was a thankless job. But Nixon knew his job and how to turn the nasty fracas and publicity around: give the reporters and photographers something to write about and point their cameras at. Penn thought the suggestion was preposterous. The prince and the princess weren't posing. Or talking. Nixon, who in hindsight was proved correct, suggested that the film needed every help it could get. He was sacked. His comment? "Penn is a very aggressive, arrogant little shit."

In several corners of the world, Nixon would be hard put to find an argument about that remark: especially on the set of *Shanghai Surprise*. Personality problems also affected the cast. Penn had veteran British actor Bernard Hill removed from the film saying that he was not right for the role. A crew member on the film remembers it differently. "The problem was, Hill was too good and too macho for Penn." Also, Madonna was attracted by the strong-minded Brit known for the UK television series "The Black Stuff."

But Madonna was still standing by her man, while at the same time reading everything she could about Evita, which was about the only distraction she could enjoy. She was in the Oriental Hotel sauna when a female reporter cornered her and asked if she was enjoying herself in the Orient. "What? Being harassed? No. We didn't think we'd have any problems here." She was also asked about the Borrahlho incident: "That guy acted like a real jerk." But, despite the bravado, Madonna worried. This wasn't how it was supposed to be. It certainly wasn't looking like *The African Queen*.

George Harrison flew to Hong Kong to referee an increasingly more difficult situation. Madonna saw it as a test. There were big black rats under her trailer. The two-legged kind were on the streets and these Chinese gangsters began making extortion demands. Extra security men were brought in because of a death threat made against Madonna, according to a source who worked on the film. Madonna was depressed. This was only her second film. The go-for-it-I-can-do-it young girl who had conquered New York was feeling totally insecure and inadequate in a foreign land.

Penn, playing Mr. Wade, a grifter on the loose in the Orient, seemed to be staying in character around the clock and was not available to provide support for Madonna. Director Jim Goddard, then fifty, had earned his spurs in television and had been strongly recommended to Penn by Martin Sheen. He might have been able to help Madonna, but she'd seen her young husband challenge his decisions and that ruled him out as a shoulder to cry on. And neither was Harrison a help to her. Madonna regarded the quiet former Beatle as a rather sweet but hapless character. There was no father figure for her anywhere in the Orient. Under all this

On a walk to the Plaza Hotel in Manhattan for a visit with Warren
Beatty, June 24, 1990. (Randy Bauer/Galella, LTD.)

Jogging with trainer near her home in Beverly Hills, May 10, 1990. (Bob Scott/Galella, LTD.)

Leaving Hollywood's Ivy Restaurant with Michael Jackson, April 9, 1991. (Ron Galella)

With Michael Jackson at Swifty Lazar's Spago party after her performance at the 63rd Annual Academy Awards, March 25, 1991. (Ron Galella)

Helping to launch a fundraising drive for children, New York City, August 8, 1988. (Randy Bauer/Galella, LTD.)

At the American Music Awards, Shrine Auditorium, Los Angeles, January 28, 1985. (Ron Galella)

Dancing at the Palladium in New York City, June 5, 1985. (Peter Savignano/Galella,LTD.)

Madonna wearing psychedelic beads on the set of a TV commercial promoting world peace, California, October 6, 1985. (Smeal/Galella, LTD.)

Doing her "Michael Jackson" for a sold-out audience at the Sports Arena in Los Angeles during her "Blonde Ambition" tour, May 11, 1990. (Smeal/Galella, LTD.)

With Tony Troy, who appeared with her in the controversial "Justify My Love" video, 1990. (Ron Galella)

American director Alek Keshishian escorts Madonna at the screening of his film *Truth or Dare* at the 44th Cannes Film Festival, May 1991. (AP)

Madonna performs the Oscar-winning song "Sooner or Later (I Always Get My Man)" from *Dick Tracy* during the 63rd Annual Academy Awards, March 25, 1991. (Laser Photo)

emotional stress, she clung to Penn. It was them against the world, and she had never before nor would ever again get on so well with her husband.

For her, Harrison was an old-timer, someone from the past. She'd displayed such youthful arrogance before. Just before leaving New York to begin filming *Shanghai Surprise*, she and Penn had been invited by Yoko Ono to a private dinner party in honor of Bob Dylan. Wandering through Ono's apartment in the Dakota on Manhattan's Central Park West, Madonna went into the kitchen where Dylan and David Bowie where talking. When she returned to the living room, where there was a crowd chatting over drinks and nibbles, she couldn't stop herself from blurting out: "Thank God there's somebody here to talk to—there are only old folks in the kitchen."

She was about to discover how hot the "kitchen" can get as she flew off to England from Macao to continue filming.

At Heathrow Airport, the press waited for her arrival. Penn was to join her later at Shepperton Studios in Middlesex and on location at a former sanatorium near Virgina Water in Surrey. The madness began long before Madonna got anywhere near the lunatic asylum.

Libby Krall, five-foot-ten, a "minder" to Tina Turner, Tatum O'Neal, Goldie Hawn, and Liza Minnelli, and the first female security officer at the Xenon nightclub in London's Piccadilly, was asked to take on Madonna's protection on the basis that she could guard her even in the toilet. "I said thanks, but no thanks," remembers Libby, explaining: "I just didn't want the hassle." But there were enough enthusiastic male bodyguards around Heathrow. They had been told to get Madonna out of the airport quickly. No pictures. No press. And playing Garbo was, of course, the one way to ensure a rumpus. Madonna's Mercedes sent one photographer flying. MAIMED BY MADONNA shouted a headline.

The war of the press against the "Poison Penns" began and had a good run at the beginning of March 1986 because it was all quiet on other Western fronts. Bodyguards with dogs patrolled outside the sanatorium. Inside, technicians and crew members became wary of unsettling the couple after one of them was fired for asking for an autograph. And no one seemed to know where the film was going.

Because of the problems in Macao and Hong Kong, several action sequences had not been filmed. Madonna and Penn had thought they were making a love story. The producers were looking for a *Raiders of the Lost Ark*. All were to be terribly disappointed.

Madonna told Harrison that she felt she was working through the Third World War. He called a press conference for her at the Kensington Roof Gardens. For him, the scenes were a reminder of being mobbed in his Beatle days. "In the sixties, all people could do was knock the Beatles so I've been through it all myself." But Harrison admits he was astonished at the pandemonium Madonna's press conference started. He feared for their safety. Police were called to escort Madonna away. There had been one notable quote: "I have nothing to apologize for." At that time, she hadn't seen *Shanghai Surprise*. And not many people ever did.

Penn hated the film and told his friends never to see it. Madonna regarded it as a miserable experience but bounced back on the optimistic side as she always does. She had no regrets. She had learned from it. And mostly what she had learned was to take and keep control—of the work in progress, and of the press. What had begun as a game of titillating and teasing the media, now was a serious part of the business. It knocked out her plan to costar in *Blind Date*. She had been told she would have approval of her leading man. Bruce Willis, who was hot from "Moonlighting," had already been cast. That took control away from Madonna—she was out of the project. And into making her third LP, *True Blue*. She dedicated it to Penn, whom she called "the coolest guy in the universe."

All the insider talk was that Madonna was on the way out. She'd had her run as a slut rock queen, as the Boy Toy, the Pied Piper of porn, as some would have it. Then, the critics began hearing *True Blue*. Almost all the reviews talked of the *control* and character in her singing. She coproduced the album with Steve Bray and friend and record producer, Patrick Leonard, and wrote the songs with them too. She also made a few lyrical changes to a song written by Brian Elliot called "Papa Don't Preach."

The first single from *True Blue* was "Live to Tell" from Penn and James Foley's film *At Close Range*. It became a worldwide number-one hit and had much more impact than the movie. After that

Madonna all but ignored Don Johnson's invitation to sing on his new album and instead released "Papa Don't Preach" to record chart success and an almighty controversy.

Robert Hilburn, the pop-music critic of the *Los Angeles Times* and one of the most highly regarded in America, had watched the Madonna backlash build in the music world. He says *True Blue* proved that those betting against Madonna's longevity were going to lose. "All along she had shown hints of ambition and sharp showbusiness instincts that suggested she was a survivor. Some people will never take Madonna seriously, just as many never took Marilyn Monroe seriously. Novelty images—especially that of the sex symbol—are hard to erase. But talent far outshines novelty. Like David Bowie, she *visualizes* music."

And "Papa Don't Preach" could have been created for MTV. It tells the story of an unwed girl who decides to keep her baby but wants her father's approval for doing so.

Madonna delivered the song in a passionate, immediate, almost sob. It started trouble. Alfred Moran of Planned Parenthood said: "The message is that getting pregnant is cool and having a baby is the right thing and the good thing and don't listen to your parents, school, anybody who tells you otherwise—don't preach to me, daddy. The reality is, what Madonna was suggesting to teenagers was a path to permanent poverty.

"Everybody I've talked to believes she has had more impact on young teenagers than any other single entertainer since the Beatles."

The pro-lifers backed Madonna. First, Parents Resources Center founder Tipper Gore endorsed the song since it told of a woman deciding against an abortion. Next, feminist lawyer Gloria Allred and the National Organization for Women asked that Madonna speak out supporting their pro-choice view.

Madonna tried to steer away from such an emotional issue. She thought the song was about a celebration of life. Her video—with the fine actor Danny Aiello as her father—features Madonna as a shivering waif waiting for her father's answer. Waiting for Daddy's approval. Aiello calls her a "true superstar" and recalls being so impressed by her that he told her: "Madonna, I look into your eyes and I can see your heart." He says she told him: "I'm not that soft."

The song could have been written for her. It wasn't. Brian Elliot who was responsible for this landmark in Madonna's career is a bearded, jolly forty-year-old who has a studio-office close to North Hollywood High School.

My studio window is the biggest mirror in North Holly-wood—girls stop to look at their reflection, fix their hair, talk things over. Their gossip is unbelievable. I developed an em-pathy for the things they got themselves into. The girl in the song is a composite. It's a reflection of things overheard. I wrote it for another singer, but someone at Warner Brothers heard it and thought it would be perfect for Madonna. If someone else had sung it, then it would have had an entirely different resonance. But Madonna is larger than life. I didn't think of the social consequences. I knew it was freighted with all kinds of reality. But basically I wanted to write a good piece drama, something that would fit into *West Side Story.* Picture that song sung by someone waif-like and it becomes something entirely different.

It's more of a plea for compassion from the father not a "Hey, I'm going to keep my baby whether you like it or not." I thought it was very strange casting matching the song with Madonna, but it worked.

10

Jailhouse Blues

I have my insecure moments and that puts a lot of strain on people.
You take things out on the person you love and that causes fights,
alienation, grief, shrink sessions, and a lot of ca-ca.—Madonna in
1987

Ironically, in the months leading up to the "Papa Don't Preach"
debate, the gossip mill was insisting that Madonna was pregnant.
And Penn was behaving badly. In an interview for *At Close Range*,
he was asked about the helicopters buzzing his wedding and replied: "I consider myself very human and very moral and I would
have been very excited to see one of those helicopters burn and
the bodies inside melt."

You can always deny a quote. But you can't negate an incident
like the one that started the real decline of Madonna and Sean
Penn's marriage.

It happened in Helena's nightclub in Hollywood where Penn,
like Jack Nicholson and Anjelica Huston, had become a "regular."
So had musician and songwriter David Wolinski who was sitting
with a group of record executives a little after midnight that eve-

89

ning. "Hawk" Wolinski, who had worked with Madonna and played drums for Chaka Khan, was chatting away. Farrah Fawcett and Ryan O'Neal were at the bar. So were Drew Barrymore, Harry Dean Stanton, Robert Duvall, and singer Glen Frey. They all saw Wolinski go down after a sucker punch. Penn and Madonna were leaving the club when Wolinski first saw her.

The official police report on the case, released here for the first time, gives the most dramatic account of the inexplicable madness of the moment. And the worrying violence. File 86-0217877 from the Rampart police station dated April 12, 1986, and timed 00.30 hours reads:

> Victim stated at the above date and time victim was seated at a table when the singer and friend Madonna walked by. Victim stated to Madonna, "Good night." The suspect, Madonna's husband, stated: "Why did you try to kiss my wife?"
>
> Suspect then appeared to go mad and with his right fist struck victim on the left side of the face. The victim fell off chair and was on the ground. Suspect picked up a chair and started hitting victim with the chair and kicking victim while on the ground. Suspect then picked up a podium and was about to throw it on victim however was stopped by unknown citizen. Suspect then departed the location along with wife Madonna.

The next line reads:

> Injuries: Victim has bruises and swelling on left side of face. Victim further has large bruises on legs and lower body. Victim will seek meeting with his own doctor.

A follow-up report reads:

> Investigating officer spoke to the victim who stated that he was attending a private party at a club known as Helena's. The suspect's wife came to the victim's table and spoke to several members of his party as well as the victim. The victim was then approached from the rear by the suspect who accused the victim of bothering his wife and struck the victim several times with his closed fist. The victim fell to the floor

and in a semiconscious condition. He was then kicked several times by the suspect. The suspect walked over to the entry section of the club and picked up a small podium. He then ran toward the victim and attempted to strike him in the head. The suspect was stopped by several patrons. He was then forcibly removed from the premises.

Contacted Michael Ostin who was present during the fight. Mr. Ostin stated that he saw the suspect kick and hit the victim. Mr. Ostin further indicated that the victim did not fight back as he appeared dazed from the first blow.

The report reveals more than details about the incident. It shows the attitude of those around Madonna and Penn. The Michael Ostin in the police report was none other than Mo Ostin the executive vice-president of Warner Bros. Records' creative department and the same man who had lined up Madonna with Brian Elliot's "Papa Don't Preach." And rather than protecting Penn by saying little, Ostin told the investigating officers that not only had Wolinski not started the brawl, but that he was knocked out of any proper contest by Penn's surprise first blow.

People had been fired from the Madonna team just for asking for autographs. But for opening up to the police? Weeks later Ostin was still a Madonna player.

That night, Madonna had seen a colleague and friend hurt by Penn for no reason and another colleague indicate the blame without any hesitation. She talked to her psychiatrist about it all the next day.

In the meantime, other witnesses also said Wolinski did not start the fight. The matter-of-fact police blotter report of the incident gives the immediacy of the incident. It does not reflect the cold fury all those at Helena's that night saw in Penn.

Several years later, witnesses say they're convinced that if Tom O'Gara (the unknown man in the police report) had not stopped Penn from attacking Wolinski with the podium/statuette, the actor would have been facing a murder charge.

Madonna always knew just how far it could have gone that night and suffered nightmares because of it. Some of her closest friends found Penn spoiled and immature. And they were scared by his temper tantrums—one of which Madonna had just seen in full, bloody close-up.

"She seemed to be having a great time at Helena's. She was real bubbly and smiling a lot," says one of the Warner Brothers party. Madonna still records for the company so they are careful, but he added: "When Penn pulled that ambush punch, her mood changed just like that." Ryan O'Neal rushed over from the bar and tried to help Wolinski. "The marriage had been undergoing stress all the time," says an actor friend of Madonna's who called the Wolinski incident "the first real traumatic episode for her." He explained: "Wolinski was someone she knew and it really shook her up."

Despite being disturbed and shaken, Madonna contacted Wolinski and after apologizing for the attack asked him not to press charges. Wolinski said that an apology from Penn would be more in order. There was talk of an out-of-court settlement, but the Los Angeles city attorney went ahead and prosecuted Penn. Behind the scenes in the city attorney's office the mood was that Penn, be he Mr. Madonna or not, needed to be brought into line. Later, he would be fined seventeen hundred dollars and put on a year's probation, which wasn't exactly the hard-nosed treatment that the prosecutors had been talking about. However, Madonna was relieved. Penn had not been showing great restraint before his court hearing. The couple had bought an $850,000 Manhattan apartment on Central Park West earlier that year. That was the location for more run-ins with photographers. For Penn, the brawl never seemed to be over.

Madonna detests failure and that made her work even harder at her marriage. The thought of all the vulture told-you-sos around the world picking over her divorce made her cringe. But it didn't stop her from taking precautions. The Central Park West apartment was in her name only, as were the various companies she was setting up to develop projects—particularly films—for her. She still had not lost sight of *Evita*, but James Foley brought her a project initially called *Slammer*, although it was never to have the impact that title implied. It became *Who's That Girl?* a dizzy-dame movie with Madonna as a wrongly jailed ex-convict who is released to find revenge and fun. Madonna's Nikki Finn takes Griffin

Dunne's straight- arrow lawyer Loudon Trott along for the ride. It's quite a long ride and Madonna's voice grated. The critics snarled. Madonna had seen it as her Judy Holliday turn, or an homage to Cary Grant and Katharine Hepburn's *Bringing Up Baby,*—but it didn't match such lofty aspirations.

"Madonna has been made-up and costumed to look like an aspiring bag lady with the skin tones of a pneumonia victim," offered one of the more polite American critics. Her fans stayed away from the film. But they bought the album and the title-track single which became an international hit. Don't cry for Madonna quite yet appeared to be the message. She fobbed off the critics. She had learned from the film. Nikki had cleared her name and that was important. Madonna said she was always having to do that with the public.

Penn wasn't helping. He had gone out to dinner at the West Beach Café in Venice with a blond girl and had been spotted by photographers who patrol such celebrity hangouts. Why don't stars like I-want-to-be-left-alone Penn eat dinner at home? That night, cameraman Cesare Bonazza wished he had. He claims that after he took some pictures of Penn and the unknown girl, the actor chased after him in his truck. "He jumped from the truck and yelled: 'Come out of the car you motherfucker!' He reached under his T-shirt and pulled out a gun. He got in a shooting position with both hands grabbing the gun and pointed at me. He said: 'Give me the fucking camera! Give me the fucking camera!' He was crazy, a lunatic." Bonazza says he didn't take a picture of Penn threatening with the gun because he feared that the threat could turn fatal. "I couldn't believe the guy, one of these days he's going to get killed. I was just lucky to escape him in the traffic."

Another day, another brawl. This time a far more wide-reaching incident involving Penn. He was working for reformed Hollywood bad boy Dennis Hopper on the film *Colors*, costarring with Robert Duvall. Duvall and Penn played a veteran and a young-lion cop in the film about Los Angeles street gangs. For an article on the gangs, whose territory spreads across many of the sporting venues used for the 1984 Olympics, I had spent several frightening weeks on their "turf." *Colors* was to me a grand and accurate picture of the horror and squalor and violence of gang life. But to make it on location, using gang members as extras? Madonna made three very secret visits to Penn during location filming. Hopper told me:

> All the gang members knew Sean—they'd all seen *Bad Boys*. They'd say: "Hey, man, we know you're playing a cop but we don't know you know." They thought he was one of them. One of the Mexican gangs—the White Fence Gang—asked him to sign a homeboy [gang member] symbol for them. He said: "I don't want to sign that." They couldn't understand and asked him why. He said: "Because my homeboys are the Los Angeles Police Department." He was aggressive about that too.

The film's producer was the soft-spoken Robert Solo, who earlier had cast Penn in *Bad Boys*. Sitting in a Hollywood hotel, he said:

> I have always liked Sean Penn and I have always had a great admiration for him. You know, when they were making the film, they were in jeopardy a lot. I think most of the crew were carrying weapons. People were getting killed nearby while we were filming. One of the gang members we were using on the film was called "Destroyer" and Dennis asked him why. The "Destroyer" guy told him: "Sometimes I gotta do my business." Sean and Dennis didn't have any protection but their images. The gangbangers (gang members) liked them. "Hey, Sean Penn. Hey, Sean Penn." The image sticks. It's hard to remove.

Penn himself talked to me about Madonna's visits and said that even in that most violent arena he was not concerned for her or his own safety: "We all have a certain sense of our ability to be and not to be bull-shitted. I think I can pretty well tell when someone is being who they are around me and when they're not. So, if I was going to say something good about these guys it's that they stay pretty much as close to who they are no matter who they are talking to as about anybody I've ever met. That is, that everything they say is a lie." In *Colors*, Penn's cop character was called Pac Man because he ate up the streets. What was his definition of masculinity? "My definition for what?" he mugged. "I can only say for the character." Go on. "In a world full of cunts, I'm the guy that can make sure the manhood stays around. That's what."

It was during the filming of *Colors* that Penn not only landed himself in trouble, but in jail. It was in April 1987, a clear spring day out by the Pacific at Venice Beach. Jeffrie Klein, then thirty-two, a scrap-metal dealer from Orange County—an hour's drive but decades in mentality from Hollywood—was one of a couple of hundred nonunion extras getting thirty-five dollars a day to fill out background scenes along Ocean Front Walk. One scene called for Hopper to film Duvall and Penn strolling along. As they approached Klein, he took a camera from his jacket pocket and took some souvenir snaps. The camera lens was a red flag to Penn and he dashed toward Klein swearing and shouting: "What are you doing taking pictures?" Klein, six feet tall and weighing 210 pounds, explained he was an extra and that other people were also snapping pictures. "Sean Penn then spat in my face and said: 'What are you going to do now?'" Klein spat back. Penn started a series of punches to Klein's face. Three times the crowd of extras separated the two of them and three times Penn broke free and went back to the attack. Meagan Montgomery, another extra there that day, recounts: "I saw Penn try to leap over security guards and try to hit Klein on the head with his fist."

It had only been two weeks since Penn was fined and put on probation for the Wolinski incident. This was a blatant breach of probation, although Penn's lawyer Howard Weitzman, who had won freedom for John DeLorean in his drug-trafficking case, argued that his client had not broken probation. It was a real mess and Madonna was distraught. She had a husband who thought he was a heavyweight contender. He was also a champion boozer. A few weeks later he was stopped for running a red light; a blood test showed an alcohol content of just over .11 percent, then slightly over California's legal limit. The charge was reckless driving, another probation violation.

For weeks, Penn was to play cat and mouse with the press and the California authorities. And to sour the mix even more, Madonna said publicly that they were having marital problems. It looked like her marriage was going to turn out like her most recent films, a rather miserable learning experience.

Even before Penn went to court to be sentenced for his probation violations, Madonna had determined that the marriage was over. Publicly, she was still standing by him. It wasn't just to help him—it looked better. Madonna wanted to keep control of the circumstances and her fans' attitude toward her. It wouldn't look good to be dumping the Penn baggage just as he headed for prison. That could wait. What's a jail term between a couple spending most of their time apart anyway?

11

Madonnamania

Drugs never made anything easier to cope with. I don't do drugs because I like to be in control of my life.—Madonna in 1987

While Penn prepared for his court appearance and juggled his commitment to film his father Leo's *Judgment in Berlin* on location in Germany, his wife was taking total control of her career. She'd had eleven consecutive top five singles—only the Beatles and Elvis had matched that—and she wanted to build on that with her "Who's That Girl?" world tour and the release of the film. In long strategy meetings which would start at breakfast and often not finish until around midnight, she and her advisers were working on a new sweep of Madonnamania. She had trained for it. Two hours a day—every day.

Behind Fortress Malibu, there had been some additions: a dance studio and a personal home gym with a trampoline and swimming pool as well as weights and other workout tools. Madonna would take a bike out and spin up and down the Pacific Coast Highway or go for runs at Pepperdine University. She was twenty pounds lighter, trim and muscled, and her bustier was cinched even tighter. To go with the new svelte body, she had new hair—the Marilyn look. Although she was one of the best-selling recording artists in the world and the seventh highest earning—twenty-six million dollars in 1987—she was still desperate to escape her continuing image as simply a media curiosity, a bimbo who got lucky. The drive that got her through the early days was propelling her now.

Penn had got himself in a jam and he'd have to cope. For her, it must have seemed at the time that someone at Warner Bros., which was releasing *Who's That Girl?*, was psychic, for it would have just been too much had the film retained the original title of *Slammer*. Penn was sentenced to sixty days for his probation violations. There were all kinds of rows and an outcry when the California courts agreed to allow him to spend the time in two sessions so he could complete *Judgment in Berlin*. Then, he was seen at a Beverly Hills restaurant and, later, strolling down Fifth Avenue in New York with Madonna. They went to Marigold's restaurant for lunch, window-shopped along Madison Avenue, and visited a well-known lingerie shop. Penn should have been in Germany.

Arrest warrants were issued and then cancelled. The city fathers of Los Angeles demanded to know what was going on. It was all a farce. Finally, Penn did serve thirty-two days of his sentence, in the spit of a town called Bridgeport (population: five hundred) in California's Mono County near the Mammoth Lake ski country. Penn paid eighty dollars a day to go to jail there rather than do his time in the Los Angeles County jail. The food was hot but not haute, the blankets gray but not Ralph Lauren gray. In California, such sentences for bad boys and girls in show business are laughingly called "celebrity diversion programs" much as corporate offenders serve their time in open prisons known as Club Feds. Nevertheless, for an edgy, nerve-driven energy freak like Penn, any sort of confinement must have been hard to take.

Madonna was in Japan with her "Who's That Girl" tour when Penn was sentenced.

Madonnamania? More than they ever expected. Thousands of fans stood outside the stadium in Osaka. Ticket touts wanted seven hundred dollars a seat in Tokyo. Storms shut down the first show, but the fans didn't go home. They stood outside Madonna's hotel in the rain and chanted her name. On stage, she didn't disappoint. She was all energy in her clinging, skimpy black corset and fishnet stockings; then she added giant sunglasses and a feather boa over black pants. Her intense preparation showed when she used Japanese phrases to encourage the audience to sing and dance with her. Later, two geishas made her up in traditional style. In return, she taught them how to wink and blow a kiss. She jogged for ninety minutes every day and also did much sightseeing, going unnoticed under a dowdy brown wig. The Far East was more fun this time. But every day Sean Penn was on the phone.

Madonna was enjoying herself alone. The tour was a great success, and one she had worked for. It proved to her that her ethic of hard work and preparation did pay off. She thought of Penn as a dedicated and "honest" actor. But hadn't she really married her image of him? The reality of the flying fists and boozing was a wedge between them. It had sent her from their home; she had spent nights in hotels only a half-hour drive from Malibu. Or she'd take off to New York and the apartment there. But now it wasn't so easy to hang out with the gang from the past. Her days of anonymity were long gone.

Madonna made her first talk-show appearance with Johnny Carson to promote her upcoming tour. She put on a brave face and played the flirt, telling Carson, "I'm just a Midwestern girl in a bustier," and then adding, "I figured if I was going to present myself as a virgin to anyone, it should be you." Carson shot back, "I suppose there has to be a first in my life." It got the intended laughs.

But it was a sad time for Madonna. Professionally, she was getting it right. More than two million people on three continents would see her and adore her and lust after her. Privately, though, she had no answers in the weeks running up to her second wedding anniversary.

Martin Burgoyne, who had attended her wedding and with whom she had shared an apartment and her life in the New York days—he danced in her first video—had died of AIDS. He was a bartender at the Russian Tea Room when she was the hatcheck girl. When Burgoyne had been diagnosed as having AIDS, his old friend insisted on paying his hospital bills. She supported Burgoyne all through the illness. "I still cry when I think of him," she says. There were dark clouds all around.

Madonna decided to take control. The U.S. leg of her tour was to start in Miami. It took a 747 jet and a DC-7 to get the equipment from Tokyo to Florida and required twenty-three trucks to transport the specially built steel stage. It took a crew of about fifty technicians to set up. Coati Mundi, of Kid Creole and the Coconuts, was close to Madonna: "She's very conscious of how something looks. She likes to be in control of things. She pays 1,001 percent attention to everything."

Out on Turnberry Island, a hedonist getaway on the Florida waterways where onetime presidential hopeful Gary Hart was to get aboard the *Monkey Business* with Donna Rice and lose his White House chance, is where the "Who's That Girl?" tour group set up luxury camp. Madonna brought an extra person along—her husband. Penn played the suitor, plying Madonna with white roses and orchids. Even when photographers tried to move in, Penn gently eased Madonna and himself out of range. He even said "thank you" to a cameraman who asked to take his picture. Slugaholics don't reform overnight, but the riot act had been read.

Nevertheless, Penn resented the close contact between Madonna and the crew on the tour. They had their private jokes. One regular Madonna worker revealed, "We gave his wife a lot of attention and care and he resented that. Sean thought Madonna should be treated like everyone else's wife and she resented that. It always ended with everyone feeling awkward when he was around." Penn had to leave Florida, finish his film, and go to jail. The bombardment of flowers continued, and the phone calls, as Madonna performed her way across North America. One crew member says that while they were having a tactics meeting, Penn got through to the switchboard of her hotel in Washington. Madonna kept him on hold for forty-five minutes. That's control. And confidence. Penn, who had said he didn't care who wore the pants in his house as long as he took them off, might have pondered that while he was hanging on at the other side of the Atlantic.

It wasn't long before the geography changed, if not the attitude. Penn in jail in the California countryside of Mono County—strip searched, deloused, and wearing a blue prison uniform reading "Mono County Jail"—was allowed only fifteen-minute phone calls. Between the ones from his wife, he wrote a one-act play, *The Kindness of Women*, which he later directed on stage in Los Angeles. It's the story of a man involved in a stormy marriage involving sexual flings and heavy drinking. The dialogue ("You jerk," "You bitch") sounded close to home. Penn admitted to me that it was.

Madonnamania was sweeping Europe. In Britain, fans swooned and louts demanded: "Show us your tits." Bodyguards and photographers jogged along after her, not with her. She was in control this time. There would be no more *Shanghai Surprise* surprises. In France, she got involved in the politics of Premier Jacques Chirac, who for popularity reasons suddenly got interested in rock 'n' roll. "Everybody likes you very, very much," he told her. "I like you to," said Madonna. Chirac hugged her and the fun began. "Who's that girl at the side of the gentleman?" was the picture caption in the Paris tabloid *Liberation*. While an editorial about rock singers and politics asked, "Who's that girl?" and the reply was, "That girl is Jacques Chirac." The debate roared on with other papers joining in.

What astonished the people of Paris even more was Madonna's eating habits. She was actually on two baked potatoes a day and popcorn, but for a "banquet" dinner she served up clear turtle soup, avocado mousse, and a choice of white wine or Perrier. A choice? She told her dinner guest, "You didn't think I was going to sit her and watch you eat fancy food that I can't eat?"

She wasn't so selfish in the Old Country.

"Siete gia caldi?" (Are you hot?) *"Allora, andiamo!"* (Then let's go!) got her cheers of approval in Florence as the "That Girl," as the roadies now called the tour, blasted through Italy. In Turin, Madonna met members of the family of her second cousin Amelia Vitucci who gave her a painting of the original family home in Pacentro. Madonna was delighted. She did a little jump of a two-step and turned to the then eleven-year-old Giuseppe Vitucci and asked, "Do you want to dance with me?" The crowd did, but the young boy wasn't sure and showed embarrassment as he told her, "I don't know." His mother Amelia later said it was one "of the wonderful moments," and added, "Her family left Pacentro very poor. There was not work and it's magnificent that she came back

to us like that, as a great lady, a great success. Her family must be very proud."

Bambina De Guilio was then Madonna's closest relative in Italy. She was eighty-two in 1987, but has since died. She was not well enough to make the journey from Pacentro to Turin with the seven town councilmen who did. They gave Madonna a parchment proclaiming her an honorary citizen of their town. When photographers crowded around her and her distant relatives, there was no problem. Madonna turned to everyone and said: "*Formaggio.*"

While Madonna was playing to standing-room-only crowds—in Turin a dozen people were injured in the crush to ogle her—an enterprising Italian journalist went for a drink with some of the folks in Pacentro. He quoted one customer as saying over sips of grappa, "That girl sings and dances and shows her thighs. She is a *malafemina* (loose woman). No Madonna she. The devil is more like it."

It may have been simply the location, but then talk started about Madonna and a connection with organized crime. There were said to be investigations going on. But inquiries show that most police background checks carried out were done on Sean Penn. What alarm bells may have gone off during such inquiries are not on file in Detroit, Los Angeles, or New York. An investigator in Los Angeles said that he had heard the stories which said that Madonna had been bankrolled by other than legitimate sources to launch herself and that there was a long ongoing connection. In New York, the Mafia watchers and—unofficially—the investigators said there had been gossip, but nothing more than that. It is clear that there never was.

A prisoner who shared a cell with Penn says that Madonna talked on the phone with him every day. There were calls from France and Italy. But when she got back to Malibu, there was silence. She was busy. There were several heated phone chats before Madonna made it to Mono County Jail. Other inmates had got him going with stories about her being out on the town with Cher and Sheena Easton. On her first visit, they argued. Twenty minutes later, she stormed out. When Penn was released, Madonna made lots of optimistic noises. They went to a marriage counselor. She started house hunting, telling the Beverly Hills realtors of Hyland, Young, and Alvarez she wanted a place of her own. Elaine Young, once the wife of the late actor Gig Young, reveals, "There was not a question it was a place for a bachelor girl."

Then she stopped house hunting. Madonna was convinced she was pregnant. She and Penn had been celibate during her tour and his jail time. She was sure that all that self-denial had resulted in something "cosmic" and positive when they did get together. But shy of publicity about this, she had made her "medical" determination on a home pregnancy test kit. It was wrong, as her gynecologist on Rexford Avenue in Beverly Hills quickly discovered. No baby—well, then no marriage.

Sean Penn was on the road alone. As a surprised newspaperman found out.

In Los Angeles, the film critic for the *Santa Monica Evening Outlook* was driving out to the Pacific Coast from a movie screening. He saw a rather bedraggled looking chap thumbing for a lift. He stopped and asked, "Where are you going?" "Malibu," said Sean Penn, who was hitching his way around town fearful of another spell in jail if he dared to drive a car without insurance. Penn was hitting the bars of Malibu and Venice Beach. He was seen with friends and with girls. The cameramen loved this. Madonna spent Thanksgiving in New York with some of her family, but without Penn.

After being out of touch for four days, her husband turned up in New York looking for his celebratory turkey dinner with all the trimmings. The story was that instead she served him divorce papers. In reality, after discovering she was not pregnant, Madonna decided to go ahead with the divorce. When Penn turned up that Thanksgiving, she announced her decision, but did not start talking to lawyers until the following week. She went public with it too, saying the divorce was not the result of one incident but "a series of cumulative pressures." Liz Rosenberg, the Warner Bros. publicity person who has supported Madonna for years, then explained, "There were so many moments in their marriage when it was shaky that Madonna was finally forced to face the reality of the situation—that they weren't happy together."

The best career move since losing her virginity, laughed the wags. Loyal Rosenberg rebutted, "She wanted the marriage to work. All the jokes about the marriage motivated her to work hard at making the marriage go. I don't think she considered him in terms of her career."

An unhappy Penn loped off to Los Angeles. Madonna stayed with her sister Paula in Brooklyn. Penn went to Helena's. British singer Billy Idol was at the bar with photographer Vinnie Zuffante (Penn had hit him the previous year), and as drinks went down, Penn's ire went up. Finally, he demanded that Helena, a dark-haired Greek woman careful of her celebrity clientele, throw Zuffante out even though Zuffante was without a camera. Penn then went off to the bathroom but saw the line and decided against waiting. He went outside and peed against the wall of the building. It was certainly a different way for Penn to drown his sorrows. And probably the best way, for within a couple of weeks Madonna dropped the divorce action. And Penn would sit in the Hollywood hotel saying of the lawsuit: "The divorce was more for the magazines than reality. Making any family work is an endless job that's hard enough when the family isn't public." But for a couple who had married their images it had been, as Penn was to discover, rather like peeing into the wind, despite the efforts of James Foley.

It was Foley who had brought about the reconciliation. The director who had worked with, and for, Penn and Madonna, admired both in their separate ways. While the lawsuit was still being pursued, the couple began talking on the telephone. Their conversations got longer. Foley encouraged the reconciliation. Then, Penn promised Madonna something he had always written off as simply for wimps. He would see a marriage counselor whenever she wanted him to. The boozing would stop, the punching days were over . . . this was a promise, her anything reconciliation. Over Christmas, they renewed their marriage vows. It was their last happy Christmas together. And it was going to be a rocky New Year for the woman who had become one of the best known entertainers in the world.

12

Bad Memories

I could never live a sheltered life—that would drive me insane.
—Madonna in 1988

The rains came early to southern California in 1988. The storm clouds swept in from the Pacific one after the other as Madonna tried to settle back into marriage and take control again of her career. Her annual pretax earnings were around twenty-five million dollars, and Harry Scolinos, a Los Angeles lawyer who was involved in a lawsuit with her, offered, "I'd take her street-smart business sense over someone with a Harvard MBA any day. What she lacks in a formal business education, she more than makes up for with street smarts." Madonna's discipline is that of a workaholic. Her appearance is a business asset—she works out for three hours every day. There are the hours to be creative, to write songs, to work out routines, to read film scripts, to plan tours. There are hours for business on her fax machines and multiline Merlin phone systems. But were there also enough hours in the day for her marriage?

She and Penn were certainly trying. But whether they were star-crossed or not, they could not stay away from publicity. And it wasn't anything to do with them. First, truck driver Steven Stillbower drove his pickup through the front gate of their Malibu estate. He wanted to "see" Madonna. Penn made a citizen's arrest. More worrying was an incident when the couple arrived home with her brother Mario at 12:30 A.M. They had been grocery shopping—at the all-night supermarket on Pacific Coast Highway—and found five people wandering around their property. Penn drove Madonna to the main house where she called the police. He drove back to close the gates and at the same time called the police on his car phone. Mario drove another car down to the gates to back up Penn. Malibu Deputy Sheriff Bill Wehner recalls the evening: "Sean, with the help of Mario, approached these guys and attempted to stop them. One of them tried to punch Sean, and Sean, looking to defend himself, found a bottle of tofu salad dressing he had just bought and hit the guy with it."

When the police reporters discovered the incident, the salad-dressing-Sean-Penn-brawl got the actor some of the most positive publicity he'd ever had. But it was still publicity and more evidence that *whatever* happened in their lives would go on in the public spotlight.

Even Madonna's morbid fear of death was to become painfully public. She never expected to live longer than her mother whom she had watched suffer and die so painfully from breast cancer. When Madonna discovered a lump on her left breast, she panicked. Initially she did the right thing and went for an examination. There were uneasy minutes in the Southwest-style reception room of Dr. Jerrold Steiner, the cancer specialist who treated Sammy Davis, Jr. and Gilda Radner.

Steiner, a soft-spoken man with a salt-and-pepper beard, spent twenty minutes explaining the problems and treatments available for breast cancer before examining Madonna. After the examination, he asked Madonna to return in two weeks for another checkup and test at the Cedars-Sinai Hospital in Los Angeles. For the first time in her life, Madonna ran away from the confrontation. She'd seen her mother waste away and the haunting memories and possibilities for her were too agonizing to deal with. Finally, after nearly a dozen weeks—months which in other circumstances could have proved fatal—she braved it out and after taking a mammogram, received from Steiner a biopsy that proved negative.

Some joy resulted from Madonna's fears.

The cancer scare brought her and Penn closer together. They entertained at home in Malibu. One of the guests was Sindre Kartvedt. A Scandinavian film writer, they considered him a serious journalist and therefore someone they could easily accept in their home. But Kartvedt says he was never really comfortable during the visits:

> They both seemed to be playing out their roles. Sean was the husband. Madonna was the housewife. And neither role fitted them. They both had opinions. They both wanted to give their point of view. In that relationship, it was clear they could never be equals. They both felt as important as each other. She always seemed to be play-acting. I think she enjoyed the role of the homemaker but that's all it was—a role. When you study her character—and there's all kinds of psychological theories—it makes me think she may have been abused as a child. All the insecurities, the need to be in control, to be the boss, fit that sort of psychological profile.

Indeed, what would Freud have interpreted from the Madonna-Penn union? It was an odd match. "I was raised to believe that when you marry someone you marry him for life. You never give up," said Madonna. She also said something which pointed to Penn's bitterness over her success:

> Sean used to make fun of me. You know, those cut-off jeans I wear? Sean would bring someone back to the house and I'd be wearing those with my hair all *yech*—I mean, I'd be looking like a hag. And he'd bring a friend in and drag me over and say, "Look at her, she's one of the richest women in America." There's a difference between being born into money and making money. I'm from a poor background and basically I'm still a working-class girl. I've been known to wash a dish or two, make a bed or two.

Penn was to go off to Thailand to costar with Michael J. Fox in *Casualties of War*, a Vietnam drama to be directed by Brian De Palma. Penn said he would miss his wife but sighed: "But we've been through worse things than that, I guess."

Had they?

Credibility was what they both desperately wanted.

Madonna was a big star and a big earner, but she still wanted to prove she could act, and decided the place to prove it was on Broadway where they have been known to butcher veteran stage stars overnight. She had been a longtime fan of playwright (and film screenwriter and director) David Mamet. She had enjoyed his *Glengarry Glen Ross*, but it was when she saw his film *House of Cards* that she decided he was a "genius" and "I knew I had to work with this man." She went out and auditioned with more than three hundred other would-be Broadway stars for the three-character drama *Speed-the-Plow*. Ron Silver and Mamet-regular Joe Mantegna had already been cast as a pair of Hollywood sharks hustling a film deal. The female role is of a secretary "temp" who becomes a pawn in a power game.

"I'd wake up every morning with butterflies in my stomach," recalls Madonna of the days of *Speed-the-Plow*. The tickets were thirty-five dollars apiece—twice what Madonna fans would pay to see her in concert—for an orchestra seat at the Royal Theatre in New York. In the preview week, the place was packed. Madonna on the Great White Way brought out autograph hunters, hustlers, memorabilia dealers, and even theatergoers.

It was fifteen minutes into the play before Madonna appeared on stage carrying a coffee tray. A dozen months earlier, she had been parading on stage in her underwear. But here, she was in dark hair, skirt, glasses, and sensible shoes. Mantegna's character wants to take the temp Karen to bed. Silver bets him five hundred dollars that he can't. The New York papers had fun: NO, SHE CAN'T ACT shouted the *Daily News*. In Britain, *The Guardian*—what would seem the most non-Madonna of newspapers—was more enthusiastic: "She plays what looks like Mamet's version of the early Marilyn who also had an ambition to star on Broadway."

Madonna got her chance only because first choice Elizabeth Perkins had dropped out suddenly. Director Gregory Mosher had helped Madonna in her only previous stage work, as a gangster's moll in a 1986 workshop production of David Rabe's *Goose and Tomtom*. When Madonna heard Perkins was no longer going ahead, she had called Mosher and asked for an audition. "Madonna didn't Bogart her way into the role," remembers Joe Mantegna, adding, "a lot of high-powered actresses also auditioned."

There were six weeks of rehearsals and the Madonna discipline kicked in. Ron Silver recalls: "She was funny and feisty and the first one to know her lines—a professional. I liked her moxie." Vanessa Redgrave, who flew from London to see the show, sent on congratulations. Mosher says, "Madonna could have made a spectacle of herself, thrown her weight around or even tried to capitalize on her sexy image, but she didn't. She was a real actress—just right. She wasn't the Material Girl or her version of Marilyn Monroe." At the opening night party at the Tavern on the Green, she appeared wearing a pale blue dress with pearls. It had a subdued effect and designer Marlene Stewart—always one for the moment—said it was entirely intentional.

But as often with Madonna, it was an illusion. She was nowhere as cool as she looked. Throughout the run of the show she had constant changes of costume. Even the dressers remarked—and two even complained—about the smell of her costumes, the stench from the perspiration. The fear of putting herself out there—what must have been an incredible pressure—she has always dismissed as "butterflies." It may have been one of her most terrifying stage appearances, but Lindsay Law, executive producer of her next film, *Bloodhounds of Broadway*, said, "It was one of the smartest things she'd ever done."

Madonna worked with a string of established acting talents— Randy Quaid, Rutger Hauer, Matt Dillon, and Jennifer Grey—on *Bloodhounds*, which was a sort of *Guys and Dolls* romp. Screenwriter and director Howard Brookner took four Daymon Runyon short stories and set them over one night—New Year's Eve, 1928. The theme was death, near-death, and the threat of death—a black comedy. Madonna's story involved Quaid as Feet Samuels, who has agreed to sell his giant feet to a crazy doctor to pay off gambling debts. Then he learns Madonna's Hortense Hathaway loves him and life isn't so bad. He wants to keep his feet. It was a small-scale project which retains an oddball charm. Madonna says she realized about halfway through filming that something was wrong with Brookner, who was later to die from AIDS. In turn, he asked her about watching her friend Martin Burgoyne die from the same disease. The theme of *Bloodhounds* and the tragic reality—an eerie surrealism, a Fellini-esque movie—made Madonna her most reflective about sexuality. About risks. About how far you, or rather she, could go. About homosexuality. About lesbianism.

Apart from this sexual dark side, *Bloodhounds* more happily gave Madonna a friend in Jennifer Grey. Grey had just broken up with her boyfriend, actor Matthew Broderick, and with Penn on location in the Far East, there were many girls' nights out.

Grey took her new friend to a birthday party for Sandra Bernhard, the offbeat actress and stand-up comic who had slipped into the mainstream in Martin Scorsese's *King of Comedy*. Madonna liked Bernhard's cool, caustic humor and went to see her one-woman show *Without You I'm Nothing*. Much of Bernhard's act is playing out fantasies. The evening Madonna was in the audience, Bernhard told a joke about how she and Madonna survived World War III. The punch line was, Penn did not survive, which got a lot of laughs at the time because of the publicity surrounding their relationship. It was the start of an ongoing and controversial friendship with the two enjoying an active lesbian relationship. And it was Midwestern girls together. Bernhard was another escapee from Michigan, from Flint, another Motor Town sprawl. Relate? These ladies were almost related.

Sandra Bernhard provided a shoulder for Madonna through the last grueling months of her marriage. The performer, a couple of years older than Madonna and known as The Mouth That Roars, recalls how they became best friends: "I was talking to her on the phone and I said, 'I can't imagine being you.' And she said, 'I can't imagine being *you*.' I thought that was a very nice thing to say."

By now they were quite literally bosom buddies. Wearing matching sequined bras, they did a bump and grind on stage belting out Sonny and Cher's "I Got You Babe" at a benefit concert in New York. When the onstage fondling got a little too much for the celebrity audience, which included Glenn Close and Meryl Streep, the high-spirited Madonna screamed: "Don't believe those stories."

Leering, the other half of this new dynamic duo shouted into the microphone: "Believe those stories!"

Which is absolutely Sandra Bernhard's style. She doesn't light up a room—she takes it over. "I'm a control person. It's hard for me to relinquish my power. It's like my weight—I'm counting down. I want to look like I'm needy because I am. We all are. It's just what I need, I don't want.

"I need stardom. It's part of the package. I wouldn't choose it on its own but in order to do what I do, I've gotta get people to pay to see me.

"I'm coming from a million places. I create a persona—the ravenous predator."

Sandra is a great fan and a loyal friend to Madonna. "We have fun, we enjoy each other's company. What more do you want me to say about it? Yes, we're best friends. And being a best friend is always being around when your friend needs you." Bernhard says that despite their hard edge approach, both she and Madonna are "vulnerable." She confesses: "I am a serious manic depressive. I get tired of being sarcastic. People think I'm always sarcastic. I try to get off in different ways being funny, but sarcasm is very easy for me. It's the easy way to make people laugh—or being wild, being really wild. Actually, I like that better."

Bernhard did get a little irritated about some of the talk about her "close" relationship with Madonna and uncharacteristically reacted with:

> We're friends and that's it. The press just can't be happy when two cool girls like us are tight buddies—like no competition, no bitchiness, except that mock stuff we put on, kind of like Dean Martin and Jerry Lewis.
>
> By the way: Did anyone ever accuse Dean and Jerry of getting it on?
>
> No. The press have to turn it into some freaky, sordid scandal when they *should* be highlighting the fact that maybe for once, two strong women are setting a positive example for the rest of the gals—it's fine to be supportive of your girlfriends, like not all women are back-stabbing, vicious nightmares.
>
> So everyone in the press can kiss my fat butt.

I asked Bernhard about the outburst at a Beverly Hills reception. "Oh, that? Hemorrhoids, I suppose."

In 1991, Madonna also got testy about their relationship. She was also most revealing:

Sandy's a great gal. Sandy's one of my only girlfriends, really. She's one of the only girls that can take me. She's really a ballsy girl. Most girls just hide under the couch. We frighten everyone out of the room. Sandy and I have always been great friends. I think in the very beginning there was a flirtation, but I realized I could have a really good friend in Sandra, and I wanted to maintain the friendship. When I went on the David Letterman show, it wasn't exactly clear how things were going to go. But Sandy started playing up that we were girlfriends, and I thought, "Great, OK, let me go for it." Because, you know, I *love* to fuck with people. Just as people have preconceived notions about gay men, they certainly do about gay women. So if I could be some sort of a detonator to that bomb, then I was willing to do that. It was really fun. Then, of course, it went highly out of control. Everybody picked up on it, and the question was, are we sleeping together? It's not really important. The fact is that Sandra sleeps with men too, and I think maybe she's trying to find happiness in her life. Maybe she was just thinking, "Can everybody just shut up so I can find somebody to have a decent relationship with?" Sandra's one of the most open people I know. You should see her in public. She's not trying to hide anything. I think it's ludicrous that people are accusing her of being in the closet or ashamed of being gay.

The fact is, she's a great friend of mine. Whether I'm gay or not is irrelevant.

Whether I slept with her or not is irrelevant. I'm perfectly willing to have people think that I did. You know, I do not want to protest too much. I don't care. If it makes people feel better to think that I slept with her, then they can think it. And if it makes them feel safer to think that I didn't, then that's fine too. You know, I'd almost rather they thought that I did. Just so they could know that here was this girl that everyone was buying records of, and she was eating someone's pussy. So there.

While the world was fascinated by the Madonna-Bernhard-do-they-or-don't-they antics Madonna was obsessed with another story—that of *Evita*. It would drive her for the next few years.

With her Siren Films Company, she was negotiating a deal with Dawn Steel, the then president of Columbia Pictures. Madonna and Siren development director Stephanie Stephens expected to have seven films "in full swing" by 1989. The plan then was for a musical built around Madonna, dramatic roles, and a comedy.

But when director Oliver Stone, hot from *Platoon* and *Wall Street*, flew into New York, he had another offer—*Evita*. Stone arrived from California to screen test Madonna for the role of Juan Peron's wife, the "saint" who died of cancer at thirty-two. Elaine Paige and others involved in the Andrew Lloyd-Webber/Tim Rice stage spectacular were not so sure. Streisand had been mentioned for the role. Meryl Streep had made a demonstration singing tape for Lloyd-Webber and Rice. During an interview, I asked Streep to sing a few bars of "Don't Cry for Me Argentina" and she burst into a fit of giggles and said: "I can't go to London. Elaine Paige would kill me."

But Streep, who was later to be disappointed by not getting the part, shouldn't have been Paige's target. Madonna was the one in line for the role. But she told Stone she would not screen test. It was an absurd gesture. Stone, who would go on to make *Born on the Fourth of July, The Doors,* and *JFK*, is himself a strong personality. It appeared to be a Mexican stand-off. However, Madonna was determined. One day *she* would be Evita. As always, she was in the overachieving business.

She was also still trying to be Mrs. Penn. Her husband was appearing in the play *Hurlyburly* in Los Angeles and Madonna was a regular at rehearsals and would telephone much of the time. But on opening night, she was late. And she arrived with Sandra Bernhard. Later in the evening, at a Century City club near the theater, Penn was back to being the bad boy: "You cunt. How could you do this to me?" he was heard shouting at Madonna.

As 1988 headed to a conclusion, so did their fiery marriage. A former employee at their Malibu home reveals how far things had gone. They would argue all the time with Penn punching out doors and walls or taking off into the grounds to massacre rabbits and birds, "anything that moved." He twice shoved Madonna into their swimming pool. Penn had pornographic books and videos and Polaroids of him and Madonna making love—pictures kept in a tin box with photographs of his dog Hank. Penn, according to the employee, would also brag about his affairs with beach girls. Guns were hidden around the house. The maids had instructions to tell Madonna if they found any weapons.

But even with all this marital madness, Madonna was still taking care of business. She knew all about Warren Beatty's *Dick Tracy*— she had been introduced to Beatty by Penn on their first date— and called him up asking for the role of Breathless Mahoney. Within a month, she was dining at the Great Greek restaurant in Sherman Oaks just over the hill from Beatty's Mulholland Drive estate. Their dinner companion was former presidential hopeful and longtime Beatty friend Gary Hart. Madonna had got her role and her man. She'd also lost her other one.

The Madonna-Sean Penn marriage was over. Until now, the extent of her life as a "battered wife" was not known. Colleagues, friends, and associates of the couple would only talk about the wild days of their relationship with assurance of anonymity. They told fearful stories. Stories of how Madonna would always take the car keys with her so that if Penn got out of hand he was the one looking for a ride home, of how Penn's constant rages and outrageous tantrums killed any love Madonna had for him, of how they feared for her life if the rages got out of control.

They did get out of control in the dying days of 1988. Madonna had agreed to work with Hollywood's leading lothario, Warren Beatty, and even an easygoing spouse might have had difficulty with that one. Penn reacted by leaving home and moving in with his parents four miles away down the Pacific Coast. He had spent Christmas with his family and out drinking with friends. Madonna had gone to a party with some girlfriends. These were tense, estranged days.

It was just after 4:00 P.M. on December 28 when Penn broke into his own home. Madonna had allowed all the help time off for the holidays. Penn put Madonna through hours of terror. He hit her, he tied her up, and he humiliated her. He also sexually assaulted her.

Officers involved in such cases are forbidden by California law from giving exact details of only a short list of sexual offenses. These include acts against children. Others involving adults also are included. Lieutenant Bill McSweeney was with the Malibu Sheriff's Department at the time of the incident. He is now an officer with the Los Angeles County Sheriff's Internal Affairs division in downtown Los Angeles. There, in his fourth floor office, he recalled how Madonna dealt with her humiliation and terror "in a businesslike way."

Lieutenant McSweeney would not specify the sexual offenses Penn inflicted on Madonna other than to tell me: "It was a unique, specific type of violence." He did indicate it was an act where California law is constructed to protect the privacy of victims. And under Deering's Penal Code these are:

288a (Oral Copulation): When the act is accomplished against the victim's will by means of force or fear of immediate and unlawful bodily injury on the victim or another person.

289 (Penetration by any foreign object): Every person who causes the penetration however slight of the genital or anal openings of any person or causes another person to so penetrate another person's genital or anal openings for the purpose of sexual gratification by any foreign object, substance, instrument or device when the act is accomplished against the victim's will.

286 (Sodomy): Sodomy is sexual conduct consisting of contact between the penis of one person and the anus of another person.

264 (Rape): Rape is an act of sexual intercourse accomplished with a person not the spouse of the perpetrator.

Until now the stories surrounding Penn's "torture" of Madonna have told of him slapping her about, threatening to stick her head in a gas oven and to cut her hair off. She was held captive for nine hours or four days, depending on which account you accept. But McSweeney offered this view: "It was all over by the time we got there. The act had been completed."

"It was a serious matter. It was something that if prosecuted would have had great implications. It was fully explained to her what charges she could bring."

Penn could not, as Madonna's husband, have legally raped her. McSweeney indicated he would have been charged with one or more of the three other offenses.

Madonna had told Penn, who was slugging Stoli vodka from a bottle, that it was all over FOREVER. He tried to tie her to a chair in what was once their bedroom, but she got away. He grabbed her in the living room and bound her. His litany of "bitch, slut, whore" banged about her head. And then there was the most awful humiliation.

Police are not sure how Madonna freed herself. One officer dismissed a suggestion that Madonna had "seduced" her way out of the trouble explaining, "It wasn't that sort of situation." She called the police on her car phone. Later, at the Malibu Sheriff's office she appeared with her face awash in tears, her lip cut. But Lieutenant McSweeney remembers that she was, despite her ordeal, very much in control and matter-of-fact about the official complaint she made against Penn. She was, McSweeney said, detailed and determined. And it was an act covered by the privacy code. He said, "When she turned up at the Malibu office to report what had happened, half of her was dispassionate. The other half was distressed. Her face was streaked with tears. She seemed to be making a businesslike decision which she had made analytically. She seemed in control, and it's rare to find anyone who can cope like that in such circumstances. She was clearly distressed and anxious to report what happened."

There were no problems with Penn at the house. "As far as I recall, he cooperated with the officers," said McSweeney.

The case changed in a few days: "She seemed to have made another business decision. She seemed to have analyzed the whole situation and decided which was the best way to take it." Madonna had decided she did not want further humiliation—an ordeal that would be drawn out in court and fanfared by an international media circus if she pressed charges against Penn. To have made them in the first place reveals not how distraught and fearful she was, but how incredibly angry she was at the humiliation, the outrage, of being so brutally controlled.

The police wanted to take things further, but Madonna resisted their pressure and had a meeting with Los Angeles County Deputy District Attorney Lauren Weiss. The details of her assault report were sealed—until now. "Madonna asked there be no criminal charges pressed. There is no other evidence on which to base a criminal charge so there wasn't one filed," said Al Albergate, the official mouthpiece for the district attorney's office. He did not say that behind the scenes there was pressure on Madonna to proceed.

But she stood by her "business decision." On January 5, 1989, in Los Angeles Superior Court she filed for divorce citing "irreconcilable differences."

Madonna never returned to the Malibu home. Friends and help had retrieved her belongings. She never wanted to be inside the house again. Instead, she found her own $2.9 million hideaway in the Hollywood Hills. And within two weeks, she and Penn—who had all manner of criminal charges hanging over his head if Madonna wanted to play hard ball with him—had agreed on a division of community property. He kept the Malibu estate, she held on to the New York apartment. Penn got a good deal because Madonna also paid him $498,000, which was his "share" of the Manhattan apartment. He got their Southwestern and Santa Fe-style Malibu furniture, while she held on to the art deco and art nouveau paintings and sculptures. She left behind her gold wedding band inscribed *M LOVE S* in her bathroom cabinet.

The financial end of their three-and-a-half-year marriage also revealed something of the cost of living as Mr. and Mrs. Madonna, the mundane and the costly side of stardom: $22.50 to the Southern California Gas Co.; $60 to John's Rubbish Co.; $36 to Western Exterminator Co.; $88.98 to Sprint; $24.20 to the *Los Angeles Times* for newspapers; $348.42 to the telephone company; $450 for a credit card payment; $92.22 to Falcon Cable TV; $50 to Penn's mother, Eileen, for an IOU; $2,118.75 to a security consultant firm; $225.50 to Bragg's Pool Service; $3,081.61 to an insurance broker; $6,000 to a "tax-exempt fund," and $7,707.60 to a "trustee."

A lot of their spending was made through Penn's production company, Clyde Is Hungry Productions, Inc. For the month of September 1988, thirty-one checks totaling $62,223.35 were written through the company. Among Penn's checks were $125.06 to the L.A. Cellular Phone Co.; $5,425.00 to his dentist, Henry R. Dwork; $59 to the On the Rox Club on Sunset Boulevard; $700 to boyhood pal, Jeff Higginbotham; $1,829.95 to American Express; $2,026.36 to PMK, a Hollywood publicity company; $27,921.60 to Arnold & Porter, a Washington, DC law firm; $17,500 to Manatee and Co., a Los Angeles financial consulting firm; and $49 to Burbank Self Storage Co.

Madonna left the bills, Penn, and Malibu, and moved on to Hollywood.

13

The Top of the Hill

I cry when I see *The Wizard of Oz*. Every time.— Madonna in 1989

Madonna bought her new home from Allen Questrom, Chief Executive of Neiman Marcus. Her neighbors included former "Charlie's Angel" Cheryl Ladd and down the road a mile, Dolly Parton. But Madonna was alone. She was at the top of the hill—literally. But alone. By now arguably the best known entertainer in the world, she lives a ten-minute drive from Hollywood's Sunset Strip. There are a couple of tight turns that lead to a narrow street that dead-ends in a cul-de-sac and the electrified gates to Madonna's home. You can't see the contemporary-style building from the street. You identify yourself over the intercom and there's a buzz and the gates swing open. A uniformed guard—guards rotate around the clock—sits in a car and watches visitors. There's lots of

119

green around. Friends go in by way of the garage, around the 1957 Thunderbird and Mercedes 560SL, and into the house through the kitchen and breakfast area. There are lots and lots of floor-to-ceiling windows, but they face to the pool and the small garden area. From the front, you see brick wall. And it's easy to see the attraction of the mix of security and serenity. An elaborate laser security system encircles the property, and if the beam is broken, the alarms blast immediately; there is no "waiting time" to allow for mistakes.

This is not the home of a Boy Toy. It is an elegant home with an eclectic collection of furniture and art placed as much for pleasure as for effect. Everything has its place. The gowns are lined up in order. There is not one cluttered closet. The black leather jackets all hang together as do the cut-off jeans. The black kidskin gloves are together and the black coats and, of course, the black lacy corsets. So are the identical black lace-up wing-tip boots. Madonna's assistants see that notes are left on the chrome taps in the bathroom for the maid: "You have not polished enough."

To the left and right of the tiled entranceway is a different touch—Madonna's office. Bookshelves have been built in and there are desks and files with phones and Fax machines. This is where the chief operating officer of Madonna Incorporated carries out her business. When you step through from the office, you're immediately in the main room. There's the grand piano, and hung from the ceiling is a gold-framed Langlois (originally painted for Versailles) with Hermes's loins dangling down. Above the white-painted fireplace is a 1932 Fernand Léger titled "Composition." Across the room from it is a self-portrait by Mexican painter Frida Kahlo. (Madonna has emerged now as such a cross-cultural icon that when the austere *New York Times* reviewed an exhibition of Mexican art at the Metropolitan Museum, its critic made a point in the first paragraph of saying the work of Kahlo, Madonna's favorite artist, was included). A nude by Kahlo's controversial husband Diego Rivera hangs on another wall. There's a photograph of boxer Joe Louis by Irving Penn and Man Ray's nude of Kiki de Monparnasse. A Tamara de Lempicka painting hangs in Madonna's spartan, white bedroom. There is no headboard for the bed, which seems to have simply been pushed up against the wall. There's her mother's photograph and the one of her in her mother's wedding dress. You need to walk through the bathroom-dressing room to get to the bedroom. It is clean and ordered with an open shower; an eighteenth-century Italian day bed and matching chairs sit beside her weight-lifting equipment and benches in front of the back-lighted glass closets. There's something gladiatorial about the room.

There are pictures throughout the house; some by her favorite photographer Herb Ritts, others by Tina Modotti and Matt Mahurin. Madonna's fascinated by Frida Kahlo, the puzzling artist and revolutionary who became a cult figure in the late eighties—with a little help from Madonna who still plans to make a film about her. In the foyer of Madonna's home is a Kahlo painting called "My Life." It shows Kahlo's mother giving birth. The bed sheets hide her head. What is seen are her open legs and the grown-up Kahlo's head appearing from her mother's vagina. "If somebody doesn't like this painting, then I know they can't be my friend," says Madonna.

It was Madonna's brother Christopher, who is gay, who helped decorate her ten-room house. He said that they looked at twenty-four other properties before making their "find." "I wanted to avoid the overstuffed California look," he says of his work, but quickly points out: "I refuse to be called a decorator. The house has the feeling of a grand New York penthouse except the view is better and there is a pool. We both love Italian furniture. It's grand without being gaudy like French furniture. Madonna and I were very close although we had become distant for about five years. It was difficult for me to find a niche in her world. We have a certain sibling dependency and we spend a lot of time fighting. Yet, we are each other's best critics."

But by now Madonna was careful about who was doing the criticizing. She had got out of her marriage and Malibu and was now in Hollywood and, most importantly, in control. When she was starting out, America's ever-young music man Dick Clark had asked her what she wanted to do when she grew up. She shot back: "Rule the world."

Well, by now she was at least ruling her world. Stories of her tough, hardheaded attitude began circulating. Pat Leonard, who had worked on her tours and records, has this thought: "Madonna had learned that after you've been burned enough times, it's better to be a tyrant than to be a wimp and have people walk all over you."

Madonna Incorporated comprised Boy-Toy for her music business, Slutco for videos, and Siren for her films. "It's a great feeling to be powerful. I've been striving for it all my life. I think that's just the quest of every human being—power."

But in Hollywood, power has all sorts of definitions. Madonna was going to be in *Godfather III*: she wasn't. She was going to play in David Lynch's *Wild at Heart*: she didn't. She was going to reprise the Marlene Dietrich role in *The Blue Angel*: she hasn't but the project is not forgotten. According to *The Hollywood Reporter*, Dietrich has said she would like Madonna to play her in any biographical film. And *Evita* was always, always in her sights. She threw director Oliver Stone off track when she suggested she should write some new *Evita* songs with Andrew Lloyd-Webber. She maintains she was never given enough guidance about the Stone/Robert Stigwood/Lloyd-Webber project at that early talking stage. And when the word ran round that Streep had not got the part, Madonna simply shrugged that it had nothing to do with her.

Jeffrey Katzenberg is the chairman of Walt Disney Studios and one of the shrewdest thinkers in Hollywood. This is a man interested in the bottom line. Period. He does not pander to stars. He'd rather make movies with animals who don't talk back and don't bark on about how many millions they are worth. A pragmatic man. And a Madonna fan:

> She has a very secure sense of her life and her business. As far as I can tell, she's always had a vision of exactly who she is — whether as an actress or a performer or as a lyricist or as a music producer or businesswoman. And she's also had a strong enough sense of it to balance it all. She's always evolving. She never stands still. Every two years she comes up with a new way of presenting herself, a new attitude, a new act, a new design. And every time, it's successful. There is a constant genesis. When something like this happens, once, okay, maybe it's luck. Twice is coincidence. Three times is just remarkable talent. A kind of genius. And Madonna's on her fifth or sixth time.

Madonna's financial adviser, Robert Nichols, put her money into real estate and "ultra safe" investments his client/boss insisted on. Stephanie Stephens and others were involved in movie deals at Columbia. There were plans for records and tours. The performer, who had rewritten the entertainment rules of the eighties, was chasing toward the next decade—with one of the largest media campaigns ever orchestrated. Madonna signed a five million dollar deal with Pepsi-Cola which gave her more than double that amount of money in free publicity. Manager Freddy DeMann thought it a smart move: "The reason I wanted to do it was because her base audience was so much broader than what record companies generally approach. No record company would spend the kind of money Pepsi was prepared to spend." What DeMann did not expect was the tempest in the cola bottle.

On March 1, 1989, Pepsico, from its headquarters in Somers, New York, sent out word that the biggest coup in advertising history was going to happen. More than 250 million people in forty countries were going to have the delight of a song of Madonna's from her not-yet-released *Like a Prayer*. The song titled "Make a Wish" was the centerpiece of a video showing her on a trip down memory lane. As she went back to her childhood the pleasures of Pepsi would be highlighted. It was a first in many ways, but shrewd Madonna was most aware of one thing: the video being broadcast worldwide didn't just showcase the soft drink but gave her unprecedented publicity.

Todd Mackenzie was the official spokesman for the Pepsi-Cola Company and he was not lost for hyperbole: "The ad will air around the globe, all across Europe and the Philippines, Thailand, Japan, in South America as well as North America. Just about every TV set on the planet Earth will have that commercial on it."

Oh, yes, but as Freddy DeMann said when asked why he was pushing Madonna so hard: "You can't take anything for granted." Especially not Madonna. Her records were selling more than one million copies a week but you don't just pump out more of the same do you? Pepsi was riding on Madonna's popularity—it cost them another five million dollars to put the commercial on television—but she also had her video of "Like a Prayer." In it, she cavorts in a black slip, wriggles between burning crosses, kisses a black saint, and shows stigmata—the imagery is provocative and irreverent. But is it blasphemous? It was a wonderful mix—Madonna, sex, and religion—for a hurricane of headlines with which Pepsi got splashed. It was a video certain to outrage those who feel comfortable with picket signs and instinctively phone in protests, which may have been the idea from the start. In the video, Madonna enters an empty church where she is drawn to a statue of a young black man robed in white—behind bars. She lies down on a pew and is apparently overcome by a vision, while the statue comes to life. In this vision, the scenario of a recent crime is unveiled. A group of white thugs attack and stab a white woman, but a black man who comes to her aid is arrested. Madonna is then awakened from her vision by a raucous black choir marching through the church. She goes to the local jail, where she vouches for the jailed man's innocence before the police—standing at the sergeant's desk wearing only a brassiere and a slip.

Madonna sings in front of a field of burning crosses. Madonna handles the murder weapon, a knife, and suddenly is supernaturally afflicted with bleeding nail wounds in her palms. Madonna does an uninhibited, giddy little dance with a gospel troupe, and at one point gets down on her knees while a choir member puts a hand on Madonna's forehead, faith-healer style. Rather than fall backward from the healing touch, Madonna appears as if she might be about to fall out of her bra.

The video began running on MTV the day after the Pepsi commercial appeared on NBC. The picket signs went up. The phones rang—especially at Pepsico, makers of the soft drink and owners of fast food chains like Kentucky Fried Chicken. Roman Catholic Bishop René Gracids of Texas and the American Family Association called the video offensive. They called for a Pepsi and Pepsico-product boycott. Madonna went pop. Pepsi yanked the commercial off the air.

The Pepsi commercial was the first time Madonna had agreed to tout or shill a product. Michael Jackson, Paula Abdul, and sell-anything-anytime Bill Cosby could go their corporate way, but not Madonna. She feared it might compromise her artistic integrity, detract from her *seriousness*. But she did Pepsi. Why? She made the rules. She is not viewed drinking the stuff. The closest she gets is to be seen twice holding a can of Pepsi. It was a disaster for Pepsi, but Madonna got her money and forests of publicity. And did the people she offended buy records anyway?

So, did Madonna indulge in a corporate ambush? Robert Mosconi, then the senior creative director at BBDO Worldwide Advertising, worked closely with her on the commercial and remembers: "One day Madonna, who liked to joke with me, came up and said, 'Hey, Roger, are you going to have the burning cross reflecting in the Pepsi can?' And I said, 'What burning cross?' And she smiled and said, 'You'll see.' "

Asked the secret of her success, Madonna put forward her considered theory: "It comes from a rebelliousness and desire to fuck with people."

Up on the hill with her Faxes and her mighty Merlin phone lines, this empress of often-carnal commerce agreed to talk to the shoemaker Nike. Madonna was to endorse a new dance shoe. Her fee would be $4.25 million. The negotiations went on in the Hollywood Hills, but a Nike executive (sworn to secrecy) said quite literally the stumbling block was Madonna's wanting to keep her endorsement and enthusiasm at a minimum. "She wouldn't even put the damn shoes on her feet!" The deal seemed to be off. Madonna could not—nudge, nudge—understand why. She called Philip Knight, the chairman of Nike. She called and called and called. Then, her lawyers called threatening to sue for the $4.25 million even though no commercial was filmed. It ended in a stand off—if we ignore the enjoyment Madonna gets from "fucking with people."

While she was being the hardheaded businesswomen, the supposed "tyrant," it ironically turned out that *Like a Prayer* was Madonna's most personal work. Critics called it "honest." It was certainly effective. In "Keep It Together," she sings, "I hit the big time but I still get the blues." In "Till Death Do Us Part," she recalls marriage: "The bruises they will fade away / You hit so hard with the things you say / He takes a drink, she goes inside / He starts to scream, the vases fly / He wishes that she wouldn't cry / He's not in love with her anymore." On "Promise to Try," a little girl—"her face frozen in time"—is comforted by her mother. "Oh Father" is the freedom from a strict father: "Maybe someday when I look back I'll be able to say you didn't mean to be cruel / Somebody hurt you too." And there was the up-tempo "Express Yourself" which was to become her seventeenth music video. It was a thumb of the nose at the good-taste brigade who had jumped on her "Like a Prayer." It was called a carnal mini-movie, all about making love not money. She was in black—stockings, suspenders, and corset—and rolling her stomach, grabbing her crotch, and seen chained to a bed and lapping at a saucer of milk. It was, she would admit, a grand fuck-you to those who had tried to control her.

Madonna was, and is, a magnet for controversy. And others wanted some of it. Pop queen Debbie Gibson piped up, saying she was concerned about how ten-year-olds would accept the latest videos. Madonna herself stuck it to LaToya Jackson, saying a *Playboy* layout done by Michael's sister was a sign of "desperation" and bitching: "She must have had a major breast job done." It was even more fun for Madonna when LaToya answered back: "Madonna is not a lady, never has been, and never will be." Her breasts? "If I'd had them done, they'd have looked a lot better than they did in *Playboy*."

At the top of the hill it was fun, if a little lonely. Madonna was linked to many men, but there were none. the only regular overnighter was her brother, of whom she says:

Christopher's gay, and he and I have always been the closest members of my family. It's funny. When he was really young, he was so beautiful and had girls all over him, more than any of my other brothers. I knew something was different, but it was not clear to me. He was like a girl-magnet. They all seemed incredibly fond of him and close to him in a way I hadn't seen men with women.

I'll tell you when I knew. After I met Christopher [Flynn], I brought my brother to my ballet class because he wanted to start studying dance. I just saw something between them. I can't even tell you exactly what. But then I thought, *Oh, I get it. Oh, okay. He likes men too.* It was an incredible revelation, but I didn't say anything to my brother yet. I'm not even sure he knew. He's two years younger than me. He was still a baby. I could just feel something.

She talked of her family's reaction:

My father's very old-fashioned, traditional, grew up in that macho Italian world. I know he's probably not really comfortable with it. He doesn't treat my brother any differently than all of us, but I know that there's an unspoken thing where Christopher doesn't feel like he's accepted by my father. All of my other brothers and sisters certainly accept it. God knows what my father accepts in my life, you know what I mean? My father is a very silent man. He keeps a lot inside.

The only others staying over were business people, sleeping in spare rooms. Madonna paid for the best. She is America's biggest-earning female performer and her earnings are more uplifting than even the most notorious of her black bras. Since 1986—and if she's coy about any figures, it's her financial ones—she's earned around $197 million. Before taxes. She's the boss, the president of a corporation that employs hundreds ("I keep Warner Brothers in work!") and going nowhere but into more profit. For the Time-Warner Corporation, she has sold more than half a *billion* dollars worth of records—as well as the hundreds of millions of dollars more for those involved in the concerts and videos and all manner of other spin-offs.

And she is involved in *every* deal. Her lawyers and accountants are there to advise her, to tell her what to do. In return, they do well. Freddy DeMann, as her personal manager, makes ten percent of her earnings; her lawyer, Paul Schindler, of New York's Grubman, Indursky and Schindler, is regarded as a top professional and gets five percent; so does business manager Bert Pedall, who has a golden client list of past problems with illegal tax shelters. But there are contract clauses which keep these advisers within the one- to two-million dollars-a-year range—each. A tour manager gets ten percent of the box office—it could in fact cost Madonna money to tour given her elaborate productions and narrow profit margin.

Madonna knew for a long time that the way to make money in Hollywood was the movies. But only the right movies. Warren Beatty was limping away from the financial and critical flop *Ishtar* and working a longtime project for a big screen workout as *Dick Tracy*. David Geffen, who is one of America's wealthiest men from his record production companies and real estate and other investments, has been a longtime friend and adviser to Madonna. They have both been active in AIDS charities, but in more than grandstand fund-raising. Homosexuals were Madonna's first fans and she's never deserted them. When her *Bloodhounds of Broadway* director, Howard Brookner, was desperately ill in St. Vincent's Hospital in New York Madonna would make regular visits. Brookner's friend, Brad Gooch, recalls, "She was incredibly supportive—she not only visited him, but all the other patients in the AIDS ward. It was like Judy Garland visiting another sort of Oz." Madonna wanted the Hollywood end of the rainbow.

It was David Geffen who sent Madonna to a psychiatrist to deal with her emotions over her mother's death and her father's remarriage. He also sent her to Warren Beatty. He told her to call the legendary Hollywood bed-hopper, the man who could make her a movie star just like Marilyn.

Madonna got her role as Breathless Mahoney. And many prattled on about how she was working for actor's scale—the minimum wage—of $1,440 a week. What was not revealed was Madonna's business negotiations, which are now part of privileged Hollywood history, especially at Jeffrey Katzenberg's bottom-line-oriented Disney Studios. She would, in return for her services, receive "points," a good share of the box office—and video and merchandising sales. A casual estimate would put the value of all that at around seven million dollars—more than Meryl Streep makes for three movies. And, of course, there would be the fourteen million dollars from the *Dick Tracy* soundtrack album. And the "Blonde Ambition" tour—HBO paid one million dollars to televise just one concert—and other spin-offs.

Madonna has an excellent sense of sell. But how was she going to cope with get-your-pants-down-as-fast-as-possible Mr. Warren Beatty?

14

Breathless

I think 75 percent of the country wants Warren Beatty's approval.
Oh, probably 75 percent has had *him*.—Madonna in 1990

She called him "Old Man." He called her "Buzzbomb." Everyone
else called them the Odd Couple. Beatty was a challenge to Madonna. But she also saw him as a serious possibility for happiness.
He had a history. He would not be intimidated. He was cool. He
was also fifty-two when they started work on *Dick Tracy*. Beatty,
the first male sex symbol of the sixties, had been toying with the
idea of the film since 1975 and the days of Julie Christie and *Sham-
poo*. After an early meeting with Madonna about her playing
Breathless Mahoney, he and she and five others involved in the
film went for lunch at the Columbia Bar and Grill, a Tinseltown
hangout at the corner of Sunset Boulevard and Gower. South on
Gower is the "technical" Hollywood, the sound studios and the
editing rooms. That's where Beatty is happiest. Inside the Columbia, the Beatty table talked over Perrier and salads with lemon
juice dressing. It was time to go. Beatty asked if he could open an
account and the young waitress asked: "Who are you?" Madonna

said, "See, Old Man," and paid for lunch. It was a lesson in the demographics of youth and quickly learned.

"I'd seen Madonna as a very good possibility for the movie early on," Beatty told me as we talked at his work studio on Gower. But he explained, "She was not cast when we were working on the script, but it's peculiar—you write a character and then you cast a character and wonder how anyone else could have possibly played it. And you could have been turned down by fifteen people."

You can see Beatty's instant attraction for Madonna, and it's got nothing to do with bed. It has to do with work, with Hollywood, with the movies. Beatty can drop names as well as his pants. Madonna, the impatient, anxious-to-learn Madonna, wanted to hear everything. We were talking about him casting Madonna as Breathless and it brought on other thoughts:

> When I first met Faye Dunaway, I was very impressed with her. I thought she was going to be a very important actress, but I didn't think she was right for Bonnie [in *Bonnie and Clyde*]. I introduced her to Arthur [Penn] who was directing, and he immediately saw her in the part. Eventually, I could. Can you imagine anyone but Michael J. Pollard playing C.W.?
>
> I would have preferred not to have directed *Tracy*. I always prefer not to direct, but usually I go to a lot of people, and a lot of people turn me down. I didn't ask anybody else to direct *Reds* because I felt there could be problems of vision.

In *Dick Tracy* Beatty got Michael J. Pollard (as Bugs) and Estelle Parsons (as Tess Trueheart's mom) from *Bonnie and Clyde* and he considers the question of friendship longer than others:

> When you've known someone for a long time you begin to see colors and facets in their personality that you just don't see in other people because you don't know them as well. So, when you're writing you think of them. Michael J. I've known for more than thirty years. We did a play together when we were kids. I don't know if it necessarily makes me feel more comfortable. I enjoy it a lot. I see people that I've known forever. It's just that you fantasize about someone doing something and then they kind of do it. They see what you thought.

Beatty is tall and so are many of the stories about him and that's easy to understand. He's a parcel of vanity and vulnerability, a sort of paranoid Peter Pan. Which is why, when you meet him, the mind turns into a flickering film of beautiful images—a gallery of faces from a celebrity concubine revolving for more than thirty years. Madonna was one of the faces on the contemporary scene.

Beatty's other passion in life is making movies. He hasn't made many, but most have been memorable. He was the star, the producer, and the director of *Dick Tracy*, which was made for somewhere between twenty-three and thirty million dollars. It was the teaming of the tightly run corporation and an indulgent, and usually indulged, filmmaker. The result was Beatty's first box-office success in a decade and probably his biggest ever. The film—quite literally a comic strip brought to life in primary colors—is a huge enjoyment.

Beatty had been involved on and off with the project for years. When I interviewed him he sort of tottered around the editing room looking more like a college professor than a Duan Juan. He's six-feet-two with curly, slightly thinning hair which he scratches, and you can see the pitter patter of crows'-feet around those bedroom eyes.

He took off his glasses and rubbed his eyes. He had a full cup of coffee in his hand and swirled it around. For the next two hours, he would never drink from the cup. It was his prop.

"Am I a perfectionist? The positive way of saying it is that you are a professionalist. The negative way is to say you're an obsessive. The humorous way is to say you are anal retentive."

The *Dick Tracy* deal took a lot of doing. The ghosts of the forty-million-dollar bomb *Ishtar* and the critically, but not commercially successful *Reds* hovered around the negotiating table. Jeffrey Katzenberg revealed the background to what was to be Madonna's "breakthrough" movie:

We created a situation for Warren in which he was enormously rewarded for remaining disciplined to his own concept of how he was going to make the movie. I've got to give him 101 percent credit. The corridors were there but the fact is he didn't bump against the walls very often.

We must have spent two years negotiating this deal with

Warren. Warren is at his best at ten, eleven at night when I'm
at my worst. I think Warren wanted to prove to himself—and
maybe the rest of the world, but mostly to himself—that he
could take the responsibility and bring the movie in for a
price.

And what Disney got was Beatty's vision of the Chester Gould
comic strip which began life in the *Detroit Mirror* in 1931. By the
fifties "Dick Tracy" had sixty-five million readers in 550 newspapers nationwide. Gould created a rogue's gallery of colorful villains
and several of them came to life in the movie through the wizardry
of prosthetics.

There was the story that Beatty had offered Ronald Reagan the
role of Pruneface. True?

Beatty laughs. "No—but I'd have grabbed him if I could. I
would have been very happy to get him." He did get Madonna,
whose 1990 album *I'm Breathless*—as well as two other spin-offs—
were "inspired" by the film. The records were part of the marketing behemoth which the Disney people hoped would roar on and
on. (Merchandising, from Dick Tracy handcuffs and key rings and
fingerprint sets to vinyl dolls of Breathless and Tracy and coffee-
mugs-on-wheels, was wrongly anticipated as at least rivaling
1989's "Batmania.")

Beatty was the man who got up every morning and looked in the
bathroom mirror and said: *I'm* with Madonna." They were as likely
a couple as the sexy Bonnie and the sexually confused Clyde. Or
the self-important McCabe and the manipulative Mrs. Miller. But
Beatty was smitten. Madonna joined a long breakfast list that includes Joan Collins, Natalie Wood, Leslie Caron, Michelle Phillips,
Diane Keaton, Isabelle Adjani, Julie Christie, and someone in
every town somewhere. Long list? Beatty smiles: "I never talk
about anything to do with personal relationships in my life. I never
have. I don't ever intend to. If you ever see me quoted on the
subject, you'll know that someone was making it up."

Ah, the Warren Beatty legend?

These are important people to me. I don't want to hurt them
by discussing them in public. As for my love life, I can't control what other people say about; it is what it is. I know that

movie actors are overrewarded in our society and that the press has to cut people like me down to size. So they come up will all sorts of wild things. They make me into an insane eccentric with an incredible fear of losing my youth who lives in a bomb shelter, who contemplated, or who is going through, plastic surgery, who has devastating relationships with women. It goes through cycles. First they say that women like me too much; then women don't like me at all; then they like me too much again. Somewhere along the way they say I secretly like men—but then the men don't like me! I'm old. I'm young. I'm intelligent. I'm stupid. My tide goes in and out.

Madonna has now become what Beatty was in his heyday—an object of overwhelming fascination. What makes such icons tick? Is all the attention water off a superstar's back? Beatty says:

I'd like to say you develop an immunity to it, but I'm afraid it's more like an allergy. The only defense that you have is not to cooperate. The problem is that by not cooperating you give freedom to the media to invent an unlimited amount of crap, because they will do it. I have decided it's best probably not to be so circumspect about it. Not that it's likely to.... We had a very reactionary Southern senator who went to the Supreme Court and became a brilliant, articulate justice. His point of view on free speech was that all libel laws should be eliminated. There should be no recourse. At least the public would know that there is nothing you can do. The problem now is that you have to prove malicious intent and all kinds of nonsense that enables the public to think the things are 50 percent true.

But if you're a person who believes in free speech, let alone a person who doesn't want to spend their whole life and fortune fighting some sort of legal battle about what is said in the media, you ignore it.

Beatty has never married, but the warmest he would get to that subject is to talk about *Dick Tracy*: "He has primary emotions, a man who would really like to have the joys of family but is pulled by duty and doesn't know whether he can live up to the obligations of a family. He's tempted." On himself: "I wouldn't mind being married. I'd like to have children." (Beatty's comment was made before Annette Bening came into the picture.)

The Charmer

I'd like to come back as Warren Beatty's fingertips.—Woody Allen on reincarnation

Madonna quickly fell under the Beatty spell. He is *the* charmer of Hollywood. But, of course, there were all the women before her. And for all her confidence, it bothered her. Could she ever be as wonderful as Bardot at age twenty-five? Or the late Natalie Wood? Then, with her trademark positive thinking, she'd tell herself she was better than any of them. Beatty was protective and a father figure for her and certainly not easily shocked. "Warren understands the bullshit. He's been an icon for years. He's had a lot more practice at it than I have. Obviously somebody who hasn't experienced it would be more threatened by my fame than he is. You can't understand being hugely famous until it happens and then it's too late to decide if you want it or not. Warren's been a sex symbol for so long, he's just not surprised by anything." Not by Madonna. Beatty lobbed back:

I don't know that there are many people who can do as many

things as Madonna. People who are in a positive frame of mind, who bring as much energy and willingness to work as Madonna does. She has in this respect a real healthy humility about the cinema. I think this is a prime requisite to be able to function in cinema—or, actually, in art. I think she's courageous in the areas she explores artistically. I think that's what she wants to explore. I think her generous spirit would be the thing I think informs her work the most. As she goes on, she will gain the artistic respect that she already deserves. She has an unlimited future as an actress.

Beatty, true to his word, would not talk about their romantic or sexual relationship. Madonna talked about their situation: "Sometimes I'm cynical and pragmatic and think it will last as long as it lasts. Then I have moments when I'm really romantic and I think, We're JUST PERFECT together." Of course, she should have remained pragmatic. It may be difficult to imagine Madonna as the victim in a relationship, but she was about to become one—for the second time. After the divorce from Penn, she felt a complete failure. That, in time, was replaced by a deep sadness which—like a good Catholic girl—she still feels today. However, she felt it was like dealing with a death.

Dick Tracy—"Dead-eyed Dick" as the character and Beatty were known on the film set—was much more fun than the Penn days. Madonna was also involved in the music with Stephen Sondheim, the man regarded as the genius of modern musical theater. The challenge for Madonna was to get the songs across without sounding silly or false. Sondheim remembers her impatience: "She hates to make a lot of choices. For us, she did two and sometimes had to be persuaded to do three takes. It was her dancing that convinced me. I was really knocked out the moment she started to move—that's when you immediately know why she's a star."

Madonna wasn't sure she could do justice to Sondheim's songs. Everyone else—including Sondheim—was. As buttery-haired femme fatale Breathless Mahoney, she delivered. She was concerned—irked and bothered by the lack of success of *Shanghai Surprise, Who's That Girl?* and *The Bloodhounds of Broadway*— that she pull off the role. She had turned down *The Fabulous Baker Boys* which won Michelle Pfeiffer an Oscar nomination. "I hated it. It was too mushy. Such a Wonder Bread cast. I think of all these people as being Californian people—blond and boring."

The movies? I'm going to keep trying. *Dick Tracy* will help me a lot. Warren says I'm great in it and I don't think he lies about stuff like that. He's really helpful reading scripts. He has an infinite knowledge about what makes a good movie, a good director. He's a sounding board for me. He's critical and that's good.

Warren should have been a psychiatrist or a district attorney. When he wants to know somebody, he goes out of his way to investigate. You feel like you are under the microscope. You're not used to people spending that much time trying to get to know you. But it's admirable. Everybody ought to examine the people they're going to work for as intensely as he does.

I've been drawn to so many different kinds of men, I couldn't say if I've got a type. Let's say I'm attracted to men who are in touch with their sexuality—who are aware of it and who *work* it. And I prefer men who can acknowledge their feminine side. I think I have a lot of masculinity in me. Macho guys don't really go for me—certainly not when they get to know me. They're frightened of their femininity.

You imbue men with the characteristics you want them to have. Then they're not what you expect at all. But it's your own fault for not doing your homework, the investigating, the finding out. I'm more cautious now, but I'm still a hopeless romantic.

The filming and loving days with Beatty were fun. They were in restaurants all over Los Angeles. Once on a trip to New York they were heading out to Kennedy Airport and a 6:30 P.M. flight to California when she leaned over and whispered: "Let's go to Paris." The limousine driver told me Beatty didn't blink and simply picked up the car phone and made reservations.

Indulgent away from the film set, the actor-director was still the boss. And a perfectionist. Take after take after take. Al Pacino won a deserved Oscar nomination for his turn as loony bad guy Big Boy Caprice who is after Dick Tracy. In one sensational sequence he shows his chorus line, including Madonna, how to strut their stuff. Madonna remembers too well costarring with one perfectionist in front of the camera and being directed by another behind it:

> As Big Boy, he [Pacino] was always smacking my butt and my face. I hated him, I loathed him. He'd tell me the dirtiest jokes, suck on his cigar like it was some sort of weird phallic symbol, and just be a pig. So off-camera, I'd always move away from him but he'd always grab me and go: "Get over here." This is exactly what happens in the movie. Everytime I expressed my distaste for him, he'd smack me, which is also what happens in the movie. He made me cry sometimes. There was a scene where Al kept smacking me in the stomach. It would sting and what made me cry was not so much the hit, but that Warren wouldn't shout "Cut." Al just kept going and I was humiliated. And of course that was what they intended—they wanted me to show the right emotion as Breathless.

Madonna plotted revenge on Pacino, who was shy with her when they were not filming. As they rehearsed the big dance scene in which she wore a fur coat, she suddenly dropped the fake fur to the floor revealing she was naked. Pacino blushed. He didn't know where to look and only got the joke when Madonna's co-prankster Beatty burst into laughter. In another scene, Madonna walks into a room, takes off her jacket, and runs her hands down her sides. It took twenty-five takes. Perfectionist? Anal retentive?

Away from work, Madonna and Beatty were at the Catch One disco, a predominantly black-gay club where a scene from the film *Beaches* was shot, or eating at the Columbia Grill or the Great Greek and on to the funky Club Louis. "They were at all the parties—they were everywhere," remembers Lonny Roland, a Club Louis regular. They were also at Adriano's just off Mulholland up in the hills or at the popular Citrus restaurant on Hollywood's ever-so-trendy Melrose Avenue. At most places, Madonna would finally find her way onto Beatty's lap.

Madonna and Sandra Bernhard had remained great friends. They still had their "gang." As Penn was a member of the Brat Pack, the girls called themselves "The Snatch Batch." If Madonna wasn't with Beatty she was with the Batch.

On the David Letterman show, Bernhard jokingly confessed to having slept with both Sean and Madonna. And Madonna said the two of them hung out in a Greenwich Village lesbian bar known as the Cubby Hole.

I've never been to the Cubby Hole. That's the joke of it. My brother Christopher lived around the corner and I've walked by it with him and I'd sort of go, "Oh, yeah, look, there's a lesbian club." Sandra and I were just fucking with people. But then when I realized the reaction we had gotten, I, of course, couldn't leave that alone. So Sandra and I decided to tease everybody. Then, of course, it got out of hand and I didn't want to do it anymore, because it was more important for me to have a friendship. But we had our fun with that and it sort of worked itself to death.

What about, say, her relationship with Jennifer Grey? "That came out of me and Sandra Bernhard. Then it became a question of whatever female I had a close relationship with who is an outspoken girl—which Jennifer is—then I must be sleeping with her."

A waitress at Odeon, a restaurant in New York, remembers a night when Madonna and Jennifer and five other women came in for a late-night supper. "Madonna ordered a house salad and everybody else ordered a house salad. She said she didn't want dressing on it—or cheese. The others—except for Jennifer Grey who was bold enough to order cheese—said they didn't want them either. When the salads came, Madonna ate hers with her fingers; all the others ate theirs with their fingers too. Weird. And she kept looking at me. Maybe she just liked my outfit, but she was so obvious about it. Like it was a dare. Or *something*."

The hopes or fantasies, or both, of a New York waitress were far from Madonna's thoughts. She and Beatty were making the rounds. She celebrated her thirty-first birthday with him at actor Mickey Rourke's Rubber Club. She was also working and creating. Her Siren Films was making plans to film Frida Kahlo's life story—doing for the Mexican artist what Beatty did for radical writer John Reed in *Reds*. Then there were the songs for *Madonna: I'm Breathless*. Sondheim penned his three but Madonna believed hers were "the real shit." They included "Hanky Panky," which tells of the pleasures of being bound and spanked on the bottom. Madonna got the Bad Taste Attention Award again and rubbed it in by going on the Arsenio Hall talk show to say how much she likes to receive an erotic spanking. Taste? There was also the song "Now I'm Following You" with the line: "Dick . . . that's an interesting name / My bottom hurts just thinking about you." Then there was the time Beatty and Madonna slipped—forty minutes late, which is early for Beatty—into a Hollywood screening room to see a rough cut of Sandra Bernhard's film *Without You I'm Nothing*. In the movie of her stage performance, Bernhard imagines a sex session with Beatty and tells him to put on two condoms: "Oh, baby, it's no reflection on how much I care about you. We all know you've been around." Beatty and Madonna laughed together.

And in 1990 *Dick Tracy* was being filmed. Costume designer Milena Canonero wanted Madonna's Breathless to represent the night, the moon, and sex. He put her into midnight blue, silver, and black—*tight* midnight blue, silver, and black dresses. They flashily displayed Madonna's every exercised curve—one dress was cut so low, she literally fell out of it during rehearsals. Watching, Beatty smiled: "She's dressed in a way that accentuates her good health."

Her stunning figure showed she was in *very* good health. Madonna suggested she could promote *Dick Tracy* with a tour—what was to become the "Blonde Ambition" tour. "Disney didn't come to me and ask me to market the movie. Let's just say I was killing twelve birds with one stone. It's a two-way street. . . . Most people didn't associate me with movies, but I knew I have a much bigger following than Warren. A lot of my audience isn't aware of who he is."

The woman who David Geffen calls the "superstar sex goddess of the video generation" was about to go into action. And to get emotionally hurt again.

16

Madonna Inc.

As easy as it would be for me to nail a custard pie to the wall.—
Shirley MacLaine in 1991 on how easily she could cope with Madonna as a sister-in-law.

Madonna Incorporated is a smooth-running machine just like the boss of the company. She has surrounded herself with experts—in everything from music to hairdressing to stage construction. And what links them all is the Madonna Secrets Act, which works exactly like the British Government's Official Secrets Act: Those who join the firm don't talk on the record. Even platitudes. Usually. All the team works on the Madonna image and such is the confidence in the product that it now has opened up about how it gets that package ready for the road.

In just a few years, Madonna has been so many different people—the Material Girl of 1985; all Marilyn in hot pink and strapless gowns; one of the boys in 1986 with chopped hair and black cap and her "Open Your Heart"; the androgynous look in 1989 dressed in a man's suit and no shirt; the black lingerie and cross and chain woman of "Like a Prayer"; the Marilyn Monroe incarnate of 1991 bumping and grinding at the Academy Awards and belting out "Sooner or Later." That night, the talk dwelled not on Kevin Costner's Oscar wins for *Dances With Wolves*, but on Madonna and her appearance at the extravaganza with Michael Jackson. They were a couple setting down to business. The other top topic was Madonna's figure. It was the one she got for the "Blonde Ambition" tour. And you don't just wake up looking like that.

Madonna's secret is Robert Parr, a former baseball player with a crooked grin and a degree in exercise physiology. She recruited him to her team in 1987, and although he also works with Theresa Russell and Tatum O'Neal and, in 1991, with Tatum's husband John McEnroe, his number-one client and advertisement for his California-based "Up to Parr" personal trainer business is Madonna.

Theresa Russell says, "Madonna is a friend of mine. She eats, breathes, and sleeps everything in her career. It must catch up with her, even though I think she realizes it too in a way. I don't know what she is going to do. When I compared myself with her, I used to think how lazy I was, and then I realized how much I prefer my life."

Parr is, of course, more positive.

She challenges herself more than I ever could. Our workouts often start at five in the morning when she is filming. We work on stamina and endurance for her singing and dancing and we work on the shape of her body. This transformation is not an overnight thing. Madonna realizes how important her health and fitness are to her performances. She knows how she wants to look and she works hard at it. Our workouts are very focused. Doing different combinations of exercise is what creates muscle balance and avoids injuries by building up overall strength. The cardiovascular training also helps Madonna's singing by enabling her to achieve a more efficient use of oxygen. We wanted to incorporate the sinewy look. We wanted strength and endurance instead of mass and power. The advantages of working out are not only physical, they are mental. We go running or biking and then she does thirty minutes on the Lifecycle or Versaclimber—it simulates mountain climbing with the legs and arms in motion. We cool down by running stairs. Madonna then works out with ten- and twenty-pound weights. Her upper body definition comes from weight repetitions, the flat stomach is from a combination of sit-ups and pike position lifts that work the upper, lower, and oblique abdominal muscles.

The sinewy look is created with workouts and also with low body fat. Madonna is a vegetarian, and she travels with a vegetarian cook. And she drinks gallons of water to replace lost body fluids. My biggest problem is making sure she has enough complex carbohydrates and protein so she doesn't get too thin because of her workouts and her performances. We finish the workout with fifteen minutes of stretching—first the large muscle groups and then the smaller upper-body muscles.

Madonna has the genetic potential to achieve what she has and she truly enjoys challenging herself. Not everyone could look like her, but with the right, intelligent workout, everyone can look better. But it takes time and dedication to build the endurance and stamina to then create muscle tone and shape.

You change the routine for the look. Warren Beatty wanted a softer-in-the-shoulder look for *Dick Tracy*, and we did that. Then you change the intensity level a little.

When we're on tour, I go out about 6:00 A.M. and find a running course, a mix of flat and hills close to where we're staying. Then we'll run up and down the hotel stairs. I'm kinda her sounding board while we run.

Former British commando Tony Toms joined the European leg of the "Blonde Ambition" tour in the summer of 1990. By that time, Madonna's exercise regimen had taken control of her—she was addicted to it. Onlookers were sent flying as she and her entourage ran through London's Hyde Park. But it wasn't just the onlookers who were getting battered—so was Madonna's image. But she couldn't stop running. Toms reported,

She works harder than an Olympic athlete. It was frightening to see just how fit and strong she is. She had to get rid of some minders because they couldn't keep up with her. The security people think it is just a minding job until they have to go out running with her. It's then they find they can't stand the pace. We were all as fit as fiddles, but working with her still tired us out. We were knackered at the end of the tour. She is just a complete perfectionist over everything, and that includes her figure. But it is not just vanity. A Madonna concert lasts two hours and she belts out the songs nonstop while dancing around the stage. So she certainly has to be super-fit. Everything and everybody has got to be perfect for a Madonna concert. She will not put up with any slacking. If someone does something wrong, she bawls them out. But equally, she is a kind and caring person. In Barcelona, during 1990's sweltering one hundred degree fahrenheit summer, her hairdresser broke her leg in a nasty fall. Madonna was full of concern for the young girl, often bringing her presents to the hospital and sitting by her bedside. She didn't have to. The girl could have been easily replaced, but Madonna isn't like that. She's also funny. I was at the front of a group of minders surrounding Madonna and trying to push her through sixty-five hundred fans at a stadium in Barcelona. She was directly behind me hanging onto my trousers when the belt snapped and they fell down. I had nothing on underneath. But Madonna leaned forward and said sweetly: "Tony, you're supposed to hit 'em, not fuck 'em."

Australian Peter Chaplin looks after the *inside* of Madonna's body. He feeds her "performance food." Chaplin prepares a high-energy vegetarian diet and says:

Madonna is a professional and takes her fitness training and her diet very, very seriously. To keep her vegetable-fat level up, I feed her lots of avocados. I also make her drink fresh-squeezed fruit juice because the vitamins in the juice are readily absorbed. On one tour I thought up the ideal dish for her—Athlete's Answer. It's pasta with herb sauce and nuts and seeds—real training food.

On concert days, Madonna has dinner at 4:15 P.M. and I try to include recipes that give a complete protein and carbohydrate base to help her cope.

She's very up front and honest. You know where you are with her. If she doesn't like something, she'll tell you.

She likes Chaplin's food.
Here are three of her favorites:

FITNESS NOODLES
Pick your favorite noodles for this dish. It is best to use 10–12 ounces of plain noodles. Cook them according to package directions.

Be sure to keep the noodles warm while making the vegetables.

Heat 4 tablespoons of vegetable oil in a large frying pan. Add 1 pound mixed fresh vegetables (such as carrots, celery, and red peppers) cut into matchstick-thin strips.

Then add 4 teaspoons of crushed garlic, 1 teaspoon freshly ground black pepper, and 5 ounces unsalted cashew nuts.

Stir rapidly for two minutes. Place 4 tablespoons soy sauce in a measuring cup and fill with water up to 9 ounces. Add to vegetable stir-fry ingredients.

Mix well, add drained noodles. Garnish with chives or carrot strips. Serves four.

AEROBIC APRICOT CURRY
In large frying pan, cook 1 diced onion in 1 tablespoon oil. Add 2 diced carrots and 1 diced parsnip. Add 1-1/2 tablespoons curry powder, stir 1 minute. Or try Madonna's favorite spice mix: tiny amounts of lemongrass, chili, fenugreek, coriander, five-spice powder, brown and yellow mustard seeds, caraway, and ginger.

Add 2 large chopped tomatoes, a few matchstick-thin slices of ginger, and natural juice from a 15-ounce can of apricots. Simmer 10 minutes, add apricots, simmer 10 minutes. Thicken with a little cornstarch mixed in cold water. Garnish with fresh coriander, lemon juice, and tofu cubes cooked in a small amount of curry paste. Serves four.

ATHLETE'S ANSWER
On baking sheet mix 5 ounces each sunflower and pumpkin

seeds and 2-1/2 ounces unsalted peanuts. Bake in 325 degree oven 15 minutes. Mix again, put back in oven for 10 minutes. Remove, add dash soy sauce, set aside. In saucepan, boil 4 ounces potatoes. Drain, rinse, set aside. In large pot, boil 12 ounces bow tie pasta 10 minutes. Heat 1 tablespoon olive oil in small pan and saute potatoes three to four minutes. Add 2 tablespoons supermarket pesto sauce and 2 tablespoons bouillon cube vegetable stock. Drain pasta, toss in 1 table-spoon olive oil, return to pot. Add potato mixture. Mix well. Stir in nuts and seeds. Garnish with basil. Serves four.

Madonna is careful with her body—and outrageous about what she dresses it in. Her favorite designers are Jean-Paul Gaultier and Franco Moschino because she enjoys their sense of humor: "I like to cross the boundaries between men and women. That can be frightening, but the things I'm most affected by are things that frighten or challenge me. I like to nudge people, to break through stereotypes. There are too many stereotypes. Even liberated women stay in certain categories—no one is too threatening."

She's not easy to work with. Or for. Hairstylist Victor Vidal says, "She knows she's difficult, but her saving grace is that being diffi-cult is part of being honest, for her. She complains for a reason. It might be after fourteen hours of rehearsal and she'll say: "Let's get this done.' " Vidal bleached, chopped, and cropped Madonna for her "True Blue" video: "I told her about this vision I had of her. I wanted her to bleach her hair almost white and cut it short. She thought for a moment and then said, "Yes," picked up a magazine, and never looked up until I was finished."

Francesca Tolot and Joanne Gair from Hollywood's popular (with the stars) Cloutier Agency do her professional makeup. There are only two basic rules: use deeper shades of color when her hair is dark, paler shades when she is blond. "She's aware of her face—*she* knows what looks good and what does not," says Gair in a rare remark. The Cloutier Agency employees have signed the Madonna Official Secrets Act *en masse.*

Photographer Herb Ritts met Madonna in 1985 when she marched into his studio dripping in rubber bracelets, crucifixes, and other trinkets. "Her attraction isn't about her hair or makeup or clothes, it's about her evolution as a person." Or as a celebrity chameleon?

For the "Blonde Ambition" tour, the plan was for Busby Berkeley to meet Anthony Burgess's *A Clockwork Orange* with costuming by naughty Frederick's of Hollywood. The world was going to "Vogue": "I know a place where you can get away, it's called a dance floor / It makes no difference if you're black or white, a boy or a girl."

What *does* make a difference is Madonna. She has transcended all the rules of entertainment. It's that old chestnut about the telephone book—if she went on stage and read it, people would pay to see her. It's her. It is the Celebrity. Did anybody ever hear the music at a Beatles concert? We went to *see* Elvis, to *see* Michael Jackson; the Celebrity had overtaken the performer. And that was totally clear by the time Madonna strutted out on stage in conical bras and sci-fi bustiers on the "Blonde Ambition" tour. High style. High camp. Electric red lips. Dark eyebrows, the fountain of fake blond ponytail. Costumes by Gaultier and Madonna's longtime friend Marlene Stewart. Coiffed hair. Plunging necklines. Old Hollywood. Neon Las Vegas. And the corset with the pointy—back in fashion—heavily stitched bra. They went to hear her sing? Getouttahere! Madonna—number one with a bullet bra.

Madonna's latest incarnation, a twenty-first century sex siren, a Barbarella, sent her into the nineties. She'd messed with every taboo in the eighties from sex and sacrilege to cross-dressing and crucifixes so let's get going. Mimed masturbation? Yes, with "Like a Virgin." And then there were the chaps with their foot-long pointy brassieres. A touch of discipline with "Hanky Panky" and Madonna chiding: "You may not know the song, but you all know the pleasures of a good spanking."

"She said, 'Let's break every rule we can.' She wanted to make statements about sexuality, cross-sexuality, the church, and the like," recalls "Blonde Ambition" choreographer Vince Paterson, enthusiastically going on: "The biggest thing we tried to do was change the shape of concerts. Instead of just presenting songs we wanted to combine fashion, Broadway, rock, and performance art." A snappy, irreverent mongrel of a show. Paterson remembers an early conversation with Madonna: "Are you the one who had Michael Jackson grab his balls in the 'Bad' video?" she asked.

"No," said Paterson. "He was grabbing his balls before I got on the 'Bad' video."

"Well, maybe I should do it," said Madonna.

"Well, you should, because you have more balls than most of the men I know," Paterson says he told her.

The tour began in Japan. Everyone learned from the first moment who was in charge. A sound check was being taken in Tokyo and Madonna decided on a certain volume level. A technician questioned her decision and she made it clear: "Listen. Everyone is entitled to *my* opinion."

And everyone was entitled to "Vogue."

> *"They had style, they had grace*
> *Rita Hayworth gave good face.*
> *Lauren, Katharine, Lana, too*
> *Bette Davis, we love you . . .*
> *Strike a pose*
> *There's nothing to it."*

Of course, there's a lot to it. The "Blonde Ambition" tour was all part of the Madonna masterplan. She now knew she had to be pragmatic about Beatty. The closest he was to her at present was the seven show dancers in their yellow *Dick Tracy* overcoats and G-strings. Beatty's fingerprints were elsewhere. Madonna was also enjoying a quiet, comfortable love affair. Workers on the tour say she was happy and content. There were only hints as to the identity of her lover during the four-month tour and they all said he was a U.S. politician.

"*Genki Desu ka?*" shouted Madonna from the scaffolding of the Marine Stadium in Chiba as her tour of Japan began. "How ya doin'?" she followed up with as she started her tour and baptized the outdoor stadium, which is also the site of Tokyo's Disneyland. There was nothing Mickey Mouse about this enterprise.

After three weeks in Japan, the tour moved to North America, eighteen songs in ninety minutes of sellout controversy. Jean-Paul Gaultier maintains he took 350 aspirins to prepare the costumes for "the Madonna." One costume was a beaded acid-green body suit—something Cyd Charisse would have sparkled Fred Astaire with—and Gaultier says he was advised by a Folies-Bergère dresser to wash it in a "nonagressive detergent."

In Canada, there was a problem. Police were called to the Sky-dome Stadium in Toronto by parents complaining about Madonna simulating masturbation in "Like A Virgin" while lying on a red-velvet, gold brocade bed tilted toward the audience. "Morality was never involved and there was no prosecution," say the Mounties. They did admit that following complaints that the show was lewd they had agents watch it through binoculars. There's a lot of dedi-cation involved when you always get your man.

Dick Tracy was going into theaters with great fanfare. And the publicity machine was still trying to push the Madonna/Warren Beatty romance.

But this was one man, as Shirley MacLaine told me, that Ma-donna wasn't going to hang on to. Beatty doesn't want to change. At fifty-three, he's happily in control of *his* life. There's Jack and Dustin and Diane and all the others he can speed-dial on his touch-tone phone when he wants company. Madonna, the self-ad-mitted "hopeless romantic," thought she could change him. When you have succeeded at everything else it must have seemed a safe shot.

But Beatty was Beatty. He spent nights with other women. He made elaborate excuses. He fumbled and he lied about the "af-fairs." Madonna wanted a commitment. So did the world's media. She hit back at Beatty and bombarded former lover Jellybean Benitez with calls. He was staying at a West Hollywood hotel, but before midnight, he was up in the Hollywood Hills to spend the night with Madonna.

Madonna is friendly with Beatty now. She sat on his lap again at Swifty Lazar's party at Spago after the 1991 Oscars. But she re-mains hurt.

She is angry that she can't control her men. Her father's actions. Sean Penn's. Warren Beatty's. She can't take control. She doesn't want wimps, but she then can't ride herd on the ones she does want.

It's really a hard thing to accept in life that no matter what you do you can't change a person. If you say, "I don't want you looking at that woman," they're going to do it anyway. It doesn't matter what you say. You want to think that if this person is in love with you, you have control over them. But you don't. And to accept that in life is next to impossible. Then again, I want to be a fly on the wall for all Warren Beatty's conversations, but I don't want the reverse.

I'd go, "Warren, did you really chase that girl for a year?," and he'd say, "Naw, it's all lies." I should have known better. I was unrealistic, but then you always think you're going to be the one.

17

Leather and Lace

You can have all the success in the world and if you don't have someone to love, it's certainly not as rewarding. The fulfillment you get from another human being—a child in particular—will always dwarf people recognizing you in the street.—Madonna in 1991

If a week is a long time in politics, it can be an eternity in the world of entertainment. Audiences, especially Madonna's video-generation fans, want instant gratification. And, as the joke goes, they want it *now*. Madonna was seeing her psychiatrist three times a week. She seemed to have everything—and nothing. She likes everything neat like her closets: she's a symbol of the Filofax generation, her appointments and even her telephone calls are scheduled. She knows it is close to an obsession like her exercise routine and there's a Catch-22. She exercises to stop being depressed and if she didn't exercise she would be depressed about not exercising. She doesn't sleep much. In the early hours she will make lists, plan ahead.

Madonna has taken three holidays in the past ten years and was bored by the second day of each of them. She admits if she'd slowed down more she might have held her marriage together and also her relationship with Beatty. Interestingly, it is Sean Penn, who in 1991 wrote the film *Indian Runner* and directed Charles Bronson in it, who can now pinpoint Madonna as a woman of today. The film is about a returning Vietnam veteran trying to start a normal life in the Midwest.

> The film is the story of an American male's struggle. In America today there is no specific place for masculinity. There is no need to go out and hunt for food or kill the guy from the other tribe. But we've hung on to that concept and almost every guy in the U.S. has some need to live up to that tribal rite. There is nothing of value that men can do that women can't, so we are in a period of transition—trying to accept what has happened. This movie is about issues that I am trying to work out in my own life. A mature life requires responsibility and that means cutting your losses, the art of compromise.

Sean Penn on the art of compromise: certainly something completely different. Madonna would *never* compromise.

"When I lived with Sean, he loved to ball up his clothes. I'd say, 'You twisted a Versace suit into a ball and *I can't bear it.*' I would follow him and take his things and hang them up. He'd say, 'Leave me alone. I want to do it this way.' But I just couldn't stand it."

Freddy DeMann says of his number-one client: "Madonna is the biggest star in the universe. And she likes the view." Madonna admits she's stubborn: "I'm the boss. Quite frankly, a lot of things I've wanted have met with adversity. There's always this preliminary shit that's thrown and then there's my shit fit and then I do what I have to do. And they like it."

Dead-eyed Dick was over. So was the "Blonde Ambition" tour. Madonna wanted to make music. She was releasing *The Immaculate Collection*, a best-of compilation of eleven hits and two new songs, "Rescue Me" and "Justify My Love." Madonna went to France and dismayed the world's fashion editors at the Paris shows by sitting opposite them without wearing any underpants. They found it a little distracting. Herb Ritts was there taking pictures. At Thierry Mugler's third show, Madonna sat in the front row wearing a black plastic coat with fake-fur trim and a bare midriff. Two burly minders kept away the photographers. Madonna cheered Lauren

Hutton on the runway. But she also complained of the fashions: "Tired, tired—Gaultier's done that." Diane Brill got the comment: "She's soooo fat." The celebrity crowd got on their feet at the end to give Mugler, arm-in-arm with Diana Ross, an ovation. Madonna stayed in her seat. Maybe it was to save her energy. She was going to need it proving that, like her idol Marilyn Monroe's biggest film, *Some Like It Hot.*

For three days at the Royal Monceau Hotel in Paris, Madonna filmed a video for "Justify My Love." Appearing with her in it was Tony Ward, a muscled five-foot-seven model with a Roman nose, who had been Madonna's "birthday present" from her brother Mario. Ward, three years younger than Madonna, had done nude modeling and was seen wearing only a smile and an ankle bracelet in Hollywood's gay magazine *In Touch for Men.* He's also featured in Herb Ritts's book *Men and Women.* And is known at a nightclub in Manhattan that is a spot for nongay businessmen who like to relax by slipping into something comfortable after work—a cocktail dress, wigs, and makeup. Jayme Harris, a former girlfriend of Ward, claims he is a keen cross-dresser. She also said he liked whips and chains and was "quite forward about it." Now, Ward was about to get *real* exposure.

Who knows what made MTV ban the "Justify My Love" video. Maybe it was the lesbian kiss. Or the men in fishnet stockings. Or Madonna's all-but-naked bouncing bottom. Or the hints of bisexuality, cross-dressing, group sex, voyeurism, and S and M, and the full gamut of leather-and-lace sex. Or maybe it was Madonna in her skyscraper heels and scant black lingerie cavorting with Ward and kissing and nuzzling European model Amanda Cazalet. Or the insinuation of oral sex and the woman in suspenders, her nipples exposed, grasping a man's crotch. Probably most of this made MTV ban Madonna's "Justify My Love" video.

The video is populated with surreally androgynous performers. There are echoes of Visconti's *The Damned* and Cavani's *The Night Porter,* and the work of the late photographer Robert Mapplethorpe—a controversial tableaux. The message said any fetish was welcome.

So the video wasn't on MTV. Instead, it became the first video single ever released, selling at $9.98 for five minutes of entertainment. A major hit is around the fifty thousand sales mark. "Justify

My Love" was shipped out by the quarter million. In Saudi Arabia, black-market copies were selling for two hundred dollars a pop. Normally performers do not earn from videos—often they pay to make them. Madonna had made other arrangements. She had negotiated a 17.5 percent share of any sales—before it was even decided to sell the video just in time for Christmas 1990.

But it was the other business that had people talking. Who was kissing Madonna as Ward watched? Amanda Cazalet, seven years younger than Madonna, is employed by the Marilyn Gauthier modeling agency in Paris. She is a friend of rock-video mastermind Jean-Baptiste Mondino who directed the video. "It was a natural," said Robert Farrel who is Cazalet's "booker" at Gauthier, adding "Everyone knew that once Madonna met Amanda it was going to be her. They got along *very* well." Cazalet would speak only briefly about the video and Madonna: "After seeing it the first thing you want to do is make love. She knew exactly what she wanted. She had this inner power which is incredible."

No one at MTV believes that Madonna could have thought they would screen the video. American television has tough double standards. It will titillate to get ratings but it will not challenge the boundaries. The contradictions of "safe-violence" and "safe-sex" are what they practice.

Madonna appeared on "Nightline," a show that was born during the Iranian hostage crisis and has built an admirable following since then. With Madonna on the show, its ratings were the second highest in its ten-year history (fallen evangelist Jim Bakker's wife Tammy breaking down on live TV topped Madonna). But Madonna was not in control. At times she was inarticulate. But she was as bouncy as Mae West in her heyday. "You're going to wind up making more money than you would have," "Nightline" host Forrest Sawyer told her. She cheekily replied, "Yeah, so lucky me."

Of course, as Miss West knew before her, luck had absolutely nothing to do with it. Or goodness. "She gets as much out of her talent as anyone ever has," says John Branca, an entertainment lawyer who has represented the Rolling Stones and Michael Jackson. "Her major assets are controversy and sex appeal and great music."

As Branca pointed out, even Madonna's garden is controversial. Her neighbor Donald Robinson went to court arguing that her untrimmed trees ruined his view of Los Angeles. She claimed people were looking into her property. Her brother Christopher, a bodyguard, a gardener, and one of her assistants testified for her. Because of death threats, she didn't go to court. Nevertheless, sheriff's deputies screened everyone going into the Los Angeles Superior Courtroom of Judge Sally Disco, who later ruled that Madonna should trim her trees. Madonna lost. But she was going to win the big one, the film role she believed was going to make her the greatest popular star in the world.

Madonna likes to talk, but she's careful about doing so because she feels that when she talks she reveals too much of her personality. She does. Over the years, however, she has been unable to resist the urge to hold forth and, brought together, her words give a new insight into how the self-styled little girl from Michigan became a champion of so-called slut-feminism and one of the world's most famous people:

> From when I was very young, I just knew that being a girl and being charming in a feminine sort of way could get me a lot of things, and I milked it for everything I could. I think your parents give you false expectations of life. All of us grow up with completely misguided notions about life and they don't change until you get out into the world. It's like someone telling you what love or marriage is: You can't know until you're there and you have to learn the hard way.
>
> When I was a child, I always thought that the world was mine, that it was a stomping ground for me, full of opportunities. I always had this attitude that I was going to go out into the world and do all the things I wanted to do. Sometimes I travel through people, but I think that's true of most ambitious people. If the people can't go with me—whether it's a physical or emotional move—I feel sad about that. But that's part of the tragedy of love.
>
> Every time I reach a new peak, I see a new one I want to climb. It's like I can't stop. Maybe I should rest and admire the view, but I can't. I've got to keep on pushing. Why? I don't know. I don't know what motivates me. I just know I've got to do it. You have to be patient. I'm not. The more money

you have, the more problems you have. I went from making no money to making comparatively a lot and all I've had is problems. Life was simpler when I had no money, when I just barely survived.

There have been times when I've thought, *If I'd known it was going to be like this, I wouldn't have tried so hard.* If it ever gets too much, or I feel like I'm being overscrutinized, or I'm not enjoying it anymore, then I won't do it. America is really a "life-negative" society. People want to know all the underneath stuff, your dirty laundry, which isn't to say all the stuff the press has been getting on me is negative or dirty or whatever, but there's always a hope, for them, that they'll uncover something really scandalous.

You can't sit around worrying about people disliking you because they're always going to be there. It can't stop you. I could never have imagined that success could be like this. Yes, it was a surprise but I can handle it. I can still laugh about it, so I guess I'm all right. I think the ultimate challenge is to have some kind of style and grace even though you haven't got money, or standing in society, or formal education. I had a very middle-, lower-middle-class sort of upbringing, but I identify with people who have had, at some point in their lives, to struggle to survive. It adds another color to your character.

I don't like violence. I never condoned hitting anyone, and I never thought that any violence should have taken place. I have chances to vent my anger in other ways other than confrontation. I like to fight people and kind of manipulate them into feeling like they're not being fought. I'd rather do it that way.

Music is still very important to me, but I always had a great interest in films, and the thought that I could only make records for the rest of my life filled me with horror. Ultimately I want to direct films.

They thought they would wake up one day and I'd go away. But I'm not going to go away. It's more than ego. It's an overwhelming interior light that I let shine without control. I am guarded by my instinct . . . it's both my faith and conscience. I hate polite conversation. I hate it when people stand around and go, "Hi, how are you?" I hate words that don't have any reason or meaning. Also I hate it when people smoke in elevators and closed in places. It's just so rude. I have to listen to the criticism that I get when it's dealing with my work. It's beneficial, I guess. I don't take criticism very well but it's getting better. If I do something and there's one hundred people in the room and ninety-nine people say they liked it, I only remember the person who didn't like it.

I laugh at myself. I don't take myself completely seriously. I think that's another quality that people have to hold on to . . . you have to laugh, especially at yourself. I do it in most of the things I do, and most of the videos that I make, and most of my performances. Even in my concerts there were so many moments when I just stood still and laughed at myself. I am ambitious. But if I weren't as talented as I am ambitious, I would be a gross monstrosity. I am not surprised by my success because it feels natural. I'm very indecisive: yes-no-yes. In my career, I make pretty good decisions, but in my personal life I cause constant havoc by changing my mind every five minutes.

My image is a natural extension of my performance, so my songs may not be deliberately sexual, but the way I achieve them could be. Women with blond hair are perceived as much more sexual and much more impulsive . . . fun-loving but not as layered, not as deep, not serious. The artifice of being blond has some incredible sort of sexual connotation. Men really respond to it. I like to leave the impression that Marilyn Monroe did, to be able to arouse so many different feelings in people. I always acted like a star long before I was one. If people don't see my sense of humor then I come off as being expensive, but I always endear myself to people when I find their weaknesses and they acknowledge it. It's the people who try to hide everything and try to make you think they're so cool that I can't stand. I think if someone becomes hugely successful, the public becomes disgusted with them and begins to wish the star would slip on a banana peel. That's the basic aspect of human nature.

I think women are intimidated by women who are incredibly ambitious or competitive because it's easier to deal with girls who aren't. It's easier to deal with people who aren't. But I never really think consciously of the fact that I'm a girl or anything like that. In fact, I think I've had advantages because I'm a girl. . . . People say I've set back the women's movement thirty years—but I think that women weren't ashamed of their bodies in the fifties. They luxuriated in their femininity and believed wholeheartedly in it. Women aren't like men. They can do things that men can't, mentally and physically. If people don't get the humor in my act, then they don't want to get it.

The good life is to just stay in music, where I've already established myself and it's easier. I will continue to write music as long as I'm inspired. I'm inspired; I feel inspired. Just to believe in the goodness of life and to believe in yourself. That may sound silly, but that's what it really comes down to, because you can get pretty cynical about life. It's nice to be able to sit back and think that there is innate goodness in people in the world despite all the crazy bullshit that you see presented in front of you every time you read the newspapers.

I am what I am, and I do what I do. I never set out to be a role model for girls or women—and I don't conform to any stereotype. You know the idea; you need to be a chainsaw or an army tank to play in a man's world. Well, I don't act like a man, yet I play in a man's world. Irony is my favorite thing. Everything I do is meant to have several meanings, to be ambiguous. I knew I was up against a lot. I'm from a world they have no respect for. It was a really good experience for me to prove myself in that context.

There was a point in my life when I wanted to be a Peggy Guggenheim—be this patron of artists, have a gallery, and a great art collection. When I'm really, really old, that's what I want to do. She had a wild life. I like that. I've basically gone wildly out of control. My manager gets insane about what I spend. But it placates me to put my energy into that work. I could be buying a Ferrari, but I'd rather spend it this way. I think the public is tired of trying to figure out whether I'm a feminist or not. I don't think of what I'm doing as gender specific. I am what I am, and I do what I do.

There is a wink behind everything I do. The public

shouldn't think about this. Part of the reason I'm successful is because I'm a good businesswoman, but I don't think it is necessary for people to know that. All that means is that I'm in charge of everything that comes out. God! People say no to me all the time, but I guess the balance is tipped in the yes direction. If they do say no, you can be sure there will be a tantrum to follow.

I admit I have this feeling that I'm a bad girl and I need to be punished. The part of me that goes around saying "Fuck you! Fuck you! I'm throwing this in your face!" is the part that's covering up the part that's saying "I'm hurt. And I've been abandoned and I will never need anyone again." So, here—have a stereotype! I don't make fun of Catholicism. I deeply respect Catholicism—its mystery and fear and oppressiveness, its passion and its discipline, and its obsession with guilt. I hate waste and I hate to waste money. I don't see the point of having more than one car. And I hate to waste food.

Nothing that happened to me was a bad thing. Maybe I've had moments of frustration or felt that I was being misjudged, or felt that I had painted myself into a corner. But in the end, everything that happened to me was good. I get letters from guys in jail all the time, too, but they just want to have a date with me. Most people that don't like me are people that are fanatically religious.

No one can ever just play themselves in a movie. That's ridiculous. Obviously there can be a lot of things in the character that are like you, but you've got to be a little bit inventive or imaginative. I mean, there are certain things in the character that I can relate to, but I'm not playing myself, for God's sake! Yeah, but I've never been offered one [villain]. It would also be nice to play some unsympathetic characters. God knows, I have my bad side. I'm sort of naturally a pain in the ass. I naturally like to do things that rub people the wrong way. No, that's wrong. Let me rephrase that. I just like being controversial. I guess. Even that doesn't sound right. But somehow it happens that way. It's more like "Hey, well, you know how they always say things are this way? Well, they're not! Or they don't have to be."

I believe that someone is protecting me. Otherwise I'd be

dead. Otherwise that guy [I shouted at] tonight would have gotten out of his car and beaten the shit out of me. Believe me. It would have happened if I weren't protected, because I can't resist mouthing off to people when they curse at me. One time a guy did that to me and I said, "Fuck you, mother-fucker." I wasn't in my car; I was standing on the curb giving directions to my girlfriend. And this guy got out of his car. It was in the Valley. It always happens in the Valley. This big guy got out of his car and walked over to me and I was thinking, *Oh, my God, he's going to beat the shit out of me.* I was cowering. And I turned into a person I've never been in my life. I said, "I am sorry! I am truly sorry!" So I think someone is protecting me. I don't know if it's an angel. It could be the Devil. He could have his own hidden agenda.

I think most sensitive people have psychic power. I think a lot of innate psychic power has to do with just being really observant. My psychic powers show up in dreams. Or in knowing when people are going to call, or what people are going to say, or what they are going to do next. I just had dreams about being murdered all the time. The only remotely entertainment-oriented dream I ever had was one where I dreamed I kissed Robert Redford. I was in the sixth grade. And it has not come true. It was weird. I don't think I ever really had any fixation on him. But the dream was so vivid. I was really turned on. You know how you have a body spot that's sensitive or powerful? There's one for each sign. Mine is my back. I have a great back. It's beautiful, I can say that. I am not a scholar. I'm a sponge. I just soak things up.

I get a lot of bad press.

I get ripped to shreds. I've got everybody waiting to tear me down. I'm a good-for-nothing, no-talent has-been, and they can't wait until I drop dead.

Do I know what to do with my money? Yes, I do. Buy art, and invest money in writing good scripts, and give it to people who need it. Having money is just the best thing in the world. It gives you freedom and power and the ability to help other people. I know what to do with my money.

Since I was seventeen and moved to New York, I haven't

needed his [her father's] help. We're the closest when I'm in a very vulnerable state. The great thing is that when I am, he's there for me. The rest of the time I roam around the world like a miniature tank. The end of the "Oh Father" video, where I'm dancing on my mother's grave, is an attempt to embrace and accept my mother's death. My mother had a lot of us in the same month. She kept getting pregnant at the same time every year.

I had my chart done once. I remember only two things from it. One was that I should eat more cooked vegetables. The other was that I was going to meet an older man who was going to be a great influence on me. And then I met Warren Beatty. I love candy, as you can see. I'm a sugar junkie. It's because I was deprived of love as a child. I'm just kidding. I wasn't deprived. But I wasn't allowed to eat candy. That's really the reason. I've been gorging ever since I moved out of the house.

You know how religion is. Guys get to do everything. They get to be altar boys. They get to stay out late. Take their shirts off in the summer. They get to pee standing up. They get to fuck a lot of girls and not worry about getting pregnant. Although that doesn't have anything to do with being religious. Well, I moved to New York and went after my dreams. It takes a lot of devotion and discipline, and I think the combination of that and my upbringing has helped me to be as productive as I am.

You know, I can think of isolated moments where I could have given in and it would have made things better. But, all in all, I'm not with any of the people I'm not with for a much larger reason; we just weren't meant to be. If I changed and had given in, or what I conceived to be giving in, to certain concessions that people had asked of me, maybe the relationships would have been successful on the one hand, but then I would have had to give up other things in my career. And then I would have been miserable. So it's hard to say. I mean, I do look around and go, God, it's great I have fame and fortune, but then I see Mia Farrow on the set with her baby, and I think she seems absolutely content. She has a huge family and that just seems like the most important thing. And, you know, love and everything, I don't really have that, but time hasn't run out for me yet. I'm not exactly sure who I'm looking for. I wish I knew. . . . I wonder if I could ever find someone like me. . . . I would probably kill them if I did. Why is it that people are willing to go to a movie and watch someone get blown to bits, but nobody wants to see two girls kissing or two men snuggling?

I love performing, but it is very taxing to go on the road and travel in a bus. Video has made it possible to reach the masses without touring. So many people witness crimes and they're afraid to get involved because it'll only bring them trouble. They're afraid to stand out on a limb and stand up for someone else—I think it had a lot of positive messages. People have this idea that if you're sexual and beautiful and provocative, then there's nothing else you could possibly offer. People have always had that image about women. And while it might have seemed like I was behaving in a stereotypical way, at the same time I was also masterminding it. I was in control of everything I was doing, and I think that when people realized that, it confused them.

I don't think about the work I do in terms of feminism. I certainly feel that I give women strength and hope, particularly young women. So in that respect, I feel my behavior is feminist. But I'm certainly not militant about it, nor do I exactly premeditate it. So I think sex is equated with power in a way, and that's scary. It's scary for men that women should have that power—or to have that power and be sexy at the same time. I like to have control over most of the things in my career but I'm not a tyrant. I don't have to have it on my album that it's written, arranged, produced, directed, and stars Madonna. To me, to have total control means you can lose objectivity. What I like is to be surrounded by really talented, intelligent people you can trust. And ask them for their advice and get their input. But let's face it, I'm not going to make an album and not show up for the vocals or make a video and have nothing to do with the script.

Even when I feel like shit, they still love me.

I think I've met everybody.

Music is the main vector of my celebrity. When it's a success its impact is just as strong as a bullet hitting the target. Most of my lyrical ideas come from everyday life. Some are more fantasy-motivated along the lines of ideal relationships. In general, my songs are a bit of both. When you are singing a song you are making yourself very vulnerable. It's almost like crying in front of people. Acting is like that, too. It's just a different way of doing it. Everything inspires me; a great book or movie, an expression in someone's eyes, children or old men walking down the street. You know what I like to do when I go to parties? I like talking to the butler and the janitors and stuff—they're the funniest, they inspire me.

I think people have too many pretentious ideas about music . . . what's artistic and what has integrity and what doesn't. They think if it's simple and accessible, then it's commercial and a total compromise. And if it's masked in mystery, not completely understood and slightly unattractive, it has integrity and is artistic. I don't believe that. I'm sure that each record I heard influenced me in some way, just like every person you ever meet influences you.

I do in a way feel it would have been great in the old days [of Hollywood]. The studio system really nurtured and cared for you in a way it doesn't now. On the other hand, your life was not your own. Now you have more individual freedom, but you don't have anyone looking after your career in the way they did then.

So many times, I drive around in my expensive car and just think, *God, I'm just a girl from Michigan.* It all seems so strange. Because I could never imagine it when I lived there. Those are the times I feel like I'm just a girl from Michigan.

18

Hooray for Hollywood

The real secret to Madonna's success? She puts curses on people and things to get what she wants.—Anonymous letter to an American newspaper in 1991

Madonna the control freak. She says the perfect time of day, the time when she is happiest, is when the maids have gone. The bed is perfectly made, the glasses are clean, the dishes are stacked away. Everything is in its place. There is holiness in orderliness for Madonna. She *can't*, however, put on the telephone answering machine. She *needs* to answer the phone. A personal assistant travels everywhere with her; Madonna, like Cher and other popular icons, is treated like a baby. They may be tough don't-fuck-with-me-gals, but don't ask them to boil an egg. When a hand is held long enough, when an ego is stroked so much it shines, the routine of normal life gets lost. And with it vanishes a certain humanity.

Those who believe they can have anything they want make their own, often dangerous deity.

Eva Peron did. She is someone, like Monroe, who has always fascinated Madonna. And Madonna has understood the incredible screen potential of *Evita* since the success of the stage show. She fought hard to win the role.

Eva Peron went from being a brunette peasant to an upswept platinum blond and the heroine of her *descamisados*—"the shirtless ones"—of Buenos Aires. She, like Madonna's mother, died early from cancer. Evita Peron was thirty-three when the disease finally killed her in 1952. In 1979, Andrew Lloyd-Webber and Tim Rice turned the lady of the Casa Rosada, the lavish pink palace in Buenos Aires, into the unlikely subject of a rock opera. First, there was the record album, and "Don't Cry For Me Argentina" became a European hit single. By 1978 Australian entrepreneur Robert Stigwood and American director Hal Prince—who had produced Lloyd-Webber and Rice's *Jesus Christ Superstar*—staged the show in London to sensational reviews. Elaine Paige became an overnight star. As did Patti Lupone when *Evita* arrived on Broadway. It had been the most coveted—and demanding—role on Broadway since Barbara Streisand's Fanny Brice in *Funny Girl*.

Oh, what a movie it would make! A dozen actresses have flirted with the title role since 1979. Stigwood hired Ken Russell to direct a film version in Spain. Enfant terrible Russell decided Liza Minnelli should star and not Elaine Paige. Minnelli flew to London to make a test recording. "Calling it a disaster would be one of the great understatements," says Bill Oakes of RSO Films. The tape was later destroyed at Minnelli's insistence, but Russell continued to want her as Evita. RSO Films and Russell later parted company on the project in 1991.

Video director Keith MacMillan then suggested doing *Evita* by "shooting in a surrealistic soundstage environment." There would be interesting guest casting like Boy George playing the Pope. "We entertained the idea for about ten minutes," reports Oakes who said MacMillan saw the film like The Who's rock opera *Tommy.*

In the meantime, a completely separate project about Eva Peron was going on and Ronald Harwood wrote a screenplay which director Marvin Chomsky turned into the 1981 television film *Evita*

Peron. The title role was taken by Faye Dunaway. Pebbles make more waves than it did.

In 1982, *Evita* went from Paramount to Twentieth Century-Fox, then headed by Sherry Lansing, the first female to attain such a position in Hollywood. Lansing and director Herbert Ross saw the film as "a swirling, decadent fandango" and the star would be . . . Streisand or Ann-Margret. Ross then left the project (he wanted too much money) and Streisand wasn't really interested. She felt she was too old for the role. It was Jon Peters, her former-hairdresser/boyfriend turned Hollywood superpower, who wanted Streisand to play the power-mad prima donna. Stigwood was interested in Meryl Streep but found "unacceptable" Streep's condition that Mike Nichols be the director. Other directors like Alan Pakula, Francis Coppola, and Luis Puenzo were talked to and about.

Then the Weintraub Entertainment Group (WEG), headed by superbly connected Jerry Weintraub, struck a deal over financing and distribution of the film. Oliver Stone was to direct, and in the summer of 1988 he scouted locations in Argentina. He went to the birthplace of Maria Eva Duarte. "It was a lonely spot on the immense pampas where she grew up and I talked to people that still remember her. I wanted to do a film which would be beyond all political resentments and demagogic speculation."

Stone said he was considering several actresses to play *Evita*. They were an eclectic bunch: Streisand, Olivia Newton-John, and Madonna. Stone would not say if he was considering Patti Lupone.

Madonna had meetings. And meetings. She and Stone are both big egos and there were plenty of seismic tremblers from the talks as their egos snagged like the subterranean plates grinding on an earthquake fault line. Stigwood wanted Brazilian director Hector Babenco, who had won an Oscar nomination for *Kiss of the Spider Woman,* to guide the production. And he wanted Madonna as the star. Babenco was frustrated by the negotiations and had moved on to other projects.

Stone didn't like that. And that thinking had linked Madonna and Babenco. That didn't sit well with Stone who was now into the mainstream with projects like *Platoon* and *Wall Street* and was about to start work on *Born on the Fourth of July.* Stone was making a movie starring Tom Cruise, the biggest star in Hollywood at that moment. Madonna? Who needed the aggravation?

"We decided on certain things before production," says Bill Oakes, explaining: "We wouldn't dub the voice. It had to be somebody who could act and sing. Madonna asked us if she could be considered and she remained under consideration until she and Stone fell out. It would have been difficult to conceive of them working together."

Madonna felt she was kept away from the facts: was it going to be an operetta? A straight drama? A musical with dialogue? She felt she'd made enough mistakes in movies. But, although she and Stone disagreed, she was determined that one day... Madonna went on the record saying: "I've decided that if anybody is going to do it, I'm going to do it."

Stone and Meryl Streep met in the summer of 1989 and in August the Oscar-winning actress, who is also a classically trained singer, sang much of the *Evita* score. Streep, like Madonna, a hardworking perfectionist, was taking twice-weekly diva and tango lessons with singer-choreographer Paula Adbul. Stone completed the script which was described as "a politically charged love story." The original score was intact apart from one song. In Hollywood parlance "the package" of Stone and Streep was complete.

Streep's tape was sent to London. Lloyd-Webber and Tim Rice were not totally convinced. An RSO source said the praise was not lavish, but along the lines of "she can carry a tune."

Jerry Weintraub's company was having its own problems after a string of Hollywood flops like Kim Basinger's *My Stepmother Is an Alien*. Oliver Stone moved on to his Jim Morrison bio-pic, *The Doors*. Streep, ungraciously, also went through the revolving *Evita* door. She was disgruntled at wasting a year on the project. And after Madonna got what she wanted—the title role of Evita— Streep snarled: "I could rip her throat out. I can sing better than she can if that counts for anything."

Madonna had won by maintaining her stance. While others argued, she kept advertising her interest at meetings with the men that matter—the money-men known as "the suits." They sit in tower blocks and decide how to spend millions of dollars. A wrong decision and they have to find another game to play.

Madonna as Evita was certainly bankable and certainly worth a gamble. Especially for Jeffrey Katzenberg, that great Madonna fan at the Disney Studios. Since *Dick Tracy*, he and Madonna had maintained contact. Officially, the studio called it "a continuing creative agreement."

Stigwood, Lloyd-Webber, and company were now involved with Glen Gordon Caron, the creator and often the writer of *Moonlighting*. Caron would direct the film from his own screenplay which by the spring of 1991 was being called "great."

Keen at keeping the budget under thirty million dollars, the Disney people were having more meetings. But the project was "hot." Cingeri Productions, led by Andy Vajna who made a fortune with the *Rambo* films, wanted some of the action. Cingeri's films are now distributed in America by Disney, but early in the talks it was clear Katzenberg was carefully monitoring Disney's interest in *Evita*. And so was Madonna. Britain's Jeremy Irons was the actor wanted for Juan Peron. When Glenn Gordon Caron met with Irons, his title star was also present. Not only had Madonna won her role, she had negotiated conditions which gave her a say, some control, over the final film. Her time with Warren Beatty had not been wasted.

Madonna was also happy to publicly display her enthusiasm. She agreed to present Andrew Lloyd-Webber with an award saluting his work at the Los Angeles Music Center Benefactors' dinner at the Beverly Wilshire Hotel. A politically correct crowd as well as celebrities attended. Madonna arrived fifteen minutes later wearing a black sheath and platinum hair with a crowd of bodyguards snapping "Get back!" at preying paparazzi. On stage, she livened up the mainly staid audience by calling up Lloyd-Webber with: "Andrew? Where are you, you bad boy? Lloyd-Webber is bemused by his *Evita* star: "I think I'm going to have an interesting and remarkable collaboration. My goodness, she's a good girl."

Goodness, as we know, had nothing to do with it. It was hard-headed business. And Madonna was not putting all her film hopes in one production basket. She had not wasted her time waiting to get the *Evita* title role. While the negotiations were going on, she was playing an acrobat in an, as usual, untitled Woody Allen film. It sounded as though they were getting on well. He called her "prima donna" and she called him "little twerp." There were other film projects too.

In the autumn of 1991 Madonna began work on *A League of Their Own,* a film described by the producers as "about a worldly ballplayer with a sharp tongue and a fast reputation." The project first involved Debra Winger but then Madonna took the role of Mae in this story about a female baseball team in the 1940s.

Madonna decided to make *A League of Their Own* while waiting for a starting date for *Evita.* Disney Studios chairman Jeffrey Katzenberg had made a vow of film-budget austerity and the thirty-million dollar price tag for *Evita* seemed too much for him. But the Lloyd-Webber/Robert Stigwood/Glen Gordon Caron/Cannon/Madonna package remains intact and Paramount is now the likely winner in the race to make the film.

Madonna continues to cast her net around other movies. Freddy DeMann confirmed that Madonna wanted to star as the late Martha Graham, the mother of modern American dance. She also has the rights to *Little Odessa* about a Russian girl in Brooklyn. And she and Demi Moore were going to be *Leda and Swan* in an action film along the lines of *Lethal Weapon.* Madonna and Moore spent the early part of 1991 working on the script. Producer Joel Silver, who made the *Die Hard* movies with Moore's husband Bruce Willis planned two Leda and Swan sequels before the first was even filmed. Madonna as Mel Gibson? If you follow the formula, she must eventually play Lady Macbeth.

And she probably will. She's *determined* to be a major box-office movie star, a screen idol. It's in her voice. Listen: I've been a failure so far. And the reason is that I simply haven't put a lot of thought into it. I haven't honored or respected a movie career the way I should have. I didn't approach it the way I approached my music career. I'd had a lot of success in music, and all of a sudden people were going, 'Here's a movie.' And I didn't think about it. I just took it. I underestimated the power of the medium. It's been a good lesson for me.

Dick Tracy?

"You could say I have a lot of unresolved feelings about it. I remember being very upset that all of my big music scenes were cut up the way they were. I learned a lot about filmmaking from Warren, but obviously it didn't make me a big box-office star, did it?"

She'll do *everything* to make sure *Evita* does including what amounts to corporate creeping.

"There's a lot a business stuff," says Madonna about the long negotiations which she turns into a little voyeuristic fun for businessmen: "I live for meeting with the suits. I love them because I know they had a really boring week and I walk in there with my orange velvet leggings and drop popcorn in my cleavage and then fish it out and eat it. I like that. I know I'm entertaining them and I know that they know. The best meetings are with suits who are intelligent because then things are operating on a whole other level."

The suits see Madonna as the female Stallone/Schwarzenegger of the nineties.

At the Oscars, she looked like Marilyn Monroe.

She and Michael Jackson were the oddball sensation. Jackson wore *two* gloves, gold-tipped cowboy boots and a dazzling diamond brooch at his throat, his hair hanging down his back and around his often-sculpted face. Madonna was a peroxide picture in a felony low-cut pearl-encrusted Bob Mackie shimmering white gown. The twenty million dollars in diamonds—borrowed for the evening from legendary New York jeweler Harry Winston—included a thirty-four-carat pink diamond valued at fourteen million dollars which was reset for the evening into Madonna's' ring size. The baubles added extra twinkle to what headline writers were calling the date of the century in the next day's papers. Imagine if it was a *real* date—the genetic possibilities of little Madonnas and Michaels? Twinkle, twinkle little stars. But who would grab which crotch and vice versa? No. No.

It was business. Madonna and Jackson took the two front-row seats in the aisle center stage at the Shrine Auditorium. Madonna was perfectly positioned as Jeremy Irons was named Best Actor for *Reversal of Fortune.* As Irons made his way to the stage, she leaped up with a congratulatory hug and kiss eager for the celebrity audience to see how close she and the man she-wanted-to-be-Juan were. A billion people watch the Academy Awards on television: this was heavyweight public relations.

As Madonna worked this worldwide "room," Michael Jackson gazed merrily into space.

There was little space a few hours later at Spago, the now obligatory Oscar-night hangout. Wolfgang Puck's restaurant is a star spot all year, but on Oscar night agent Irving "Swifty" Lazar takes it over and it is invitation only. In 1991, Donald Trump couldn't even buy entry. Madonna and Michael waltzed in to the A-table watched by Israeli security guards. They sat with Anjelica Huston and Michael and Diandra Douglas. Al Pacino nodded to Madonna who showed him some cleavage. Jack Lemmon stared. Jeremy Irons found *Reversal* costar Glenn Close for a chat. Jodie Foster marched in wearing a breast-baring Armani jacket. Actors. Popular and honored ones. Madonna liked the company. Warren Beatty—his *Dick Tracy* took three Oscars—sat with French director Louis Malle and his wife Candice Bergen. Beatty's new lover, model Stephanie Seymour, was not with him. In a moment, Madonna was over and sniggering with Beatty and then sitting in his lap as he fondly fondled her. Michael Jackson got Diana Ross on his lap. He didn't fondle her. Madonna squealed: "It's so unbelievable. What a night!" She sounded like a girl from the Midwest. Steve Bray, the loyal, longest serving soldier on the Madonna racing team smiled: "She was always like this. She wanted attention—now it's her job."

Truth or Dare got attention. This was to home movie what *sex, lies and videotape* is to *Bambi.* The beautiful Alek Keshishian—handsome is redundant for the long-haired, brown-eyed man—directed the film. Madonna allowed him and his cameras and microphones access to almost all her waking moments, but she didn't fall for his charms: "I found Alek quite attractive, but I kept my distance because I never like to have a crush on somebody everybody else has a crush on."

The cameras didn't inhibit her. In the film she demonstrates her artfulness at oral sex by showing her gulping style on a plastic bottle of Evian water. She sings a song about farting. She ogles as two men kiss and shouts: "Oh God! I'm getting a hard-on." Later, she would reveal: "That's my favorite scene in the movie. I love that people are going to watch that and go home and talk about it all night long. I live for things like that."

There are other things to talk about. For the first time since her father's remarriage, she visited her mother's grave. In *Truth or Dare,* she lies on top of her mother's grave and wonders if her mother is "just a bunch of dust." In an unedited, three-hour black and white tape, she frolics with one of her male dancers on the "Blonde Ambition" tour and he rips off his clothes as she shouts at him: "Your cock is big." In another sequence, another dancer is reprimanded: "Get out of my bed and don't come back until your cock is bigger."

In *Truth or Dare* Madonna calls Warren Beatty "a pussy man." She appears topless. Kevin Costner appears backstage after her "Blonde Ambition" appearance in Los Angeles and tells her: "You were great. We thought it was neat." After he goes, Madonna puts her finger down her throat and says: "Anybody who says my show is neat *has* to go." Bootleg copies of the unedited documentary were selling in Hollywood for between eight and thirty-thousand dollars depending on quality.

Warren Beatty wanted some scenes of him deleted before the film went into the world's cinemas. He does nothing naughty on film—he just didn't want to be associated with it. The one Beatty scene that remained was one of the more intimate. Madonna is being examined by a throat specialist at her New York apartment. As the doctor is at work, Beatty is off-camera and muttering about the insanity of filming the medical exam. When the doctor turns and asks if Madonna wants to talk off-camera, Beatty loses his cool: "She doesn't want to *live* off-camera!"

Beatty made a point of avoiding the Hollywood premiere of Madonna's indulgent *Truth or Dare* in May 1991. He clearly didn't want to be in a situation where he might be asked to comment on the film. The special invitation-only screening at the Cineramadome was to benefit the AIDS Project in Los Angeles and the AIDS Action Foundation. The post-screening party was held at the Arena nightclub, one of the Los Angeles's most popular gay clubs. It was quite an evening.

Madonna appeared and at first was not recognized. Gone was the Marilyn-look. In its place was something closer to Morticia from television's "The Addams Family." She wore long, brown hair, a Jean Paul Gaultier cat suit and black eyeliner almost to her ears. The snake had slipped another skin. Marilyn one moment, Morticia the next.

Things were more familiar at the Arena where many of the seven hundred invited guests gathered later. Madonna's brother

Christopher was there as were David Geffen and actress Mimi Rogers (the former Mrs. Tom Cruise), Barry Manilow, Steven Seagal, Matthew Modine, Rosanna Arquette, producer Joel Silver, Vanilla Ice, and a host of enormous drag queens. Sandra Bernhard was also there. Madonna was mostly a good girl. Bernhard was her outrageous, suggestive, uninhibited self. The two girls rubbed up against each other suggestively to the delight of the Arena audience.

Truth or dare?

At the 1991 Cannes Film Festival, Madonna hosted a small dinner party where the guests played truth or dare, the game that gave her film its title. Designer Jean-Paul Gaultier dared Madonna to French kiss actress Anne Parillaud, the star of *La Femme Nikita.* She did.

Madonna was having fun publicly playing her game.

But what was even more revealing in 1991 than the film *Truth or Dare* was an interview Madonna gave to the New York-based gay magazine *Advocate.* It quickly became known as the-most-Faxed-article-in-Hollywood.

Mainstream Hollywood was amazed at what Madonna had to say. She's asked: How big is Warren Beatty's dick? And the shock was not her answer, but that she even acknowledged the question. As she did questions about whether Beatty may have gay leanings. But the big question: The Beatty dick? Her answer: "I haven't measured it but it's a perfectly wonderful size."

She admits her "agency" was "freaking" about her being demeaning in the film about Kevin Costner and she adds: "Cause Kevin Costner is like this big hero and everything. But, I mean, come on; people rip me to shreds every chance they get and I can take it, so he should be able to take it."

"Emasculating? Now, look, you can only take the balls away from people when they give them to you. I enjoy expressing myself and if I think someone is being a pussy I say it."

She was asked if she was personally kinky. "What do you mean by kinky? I am aroused by two men kissing. Is that kinky? I am aroused by the idea of a women making love with me while either a man or another woman watches. Is that kinky?" She says she has not used dildos or sex toys: "I like the human body. I like flesh. I like things that are living and breathing. And a finger will do just fine. I've never owned a vibrator."

In the *Advocate* interview she says she wants to change Michael Jackson's image. She implies that he's gay by saying that by being around her no one could stay "in a shoe box in the closet." The implication is that if they work together as they have talked about that Jackson will have to be honest.

In the same *Advocate* interview, Madonna sets herself up as a feminist heroine. A social politician? No taboo was too much for discussion.

Whether it is regarded as shameless or heroic it got the world talking about issues—and Madonna. She got jumped on and dumped on for her film and for her interview but emerged as still the world's most interesting pop icon. And the most stimulating.

But by 1991, Tony Ward, who had become her lover during and after costarring in the "Justify My Love" video, was out of her life. It seems she can always—as the Oscar song goes—get her man. Keeping him is the problem.

Epilogue

Alone on the Hill

I long for children. —Madonna in 1991

There was much talk that Madonna was pregnant with Tony Ward's child but suffered a miscarriage. She says this was never so. Tony Ward, because of his Madonna association, became the focus of much newspaper interest and it was discovered that after he and Madonna had become intimate, he married another woman. It was a marriage of convenience, pleaded Ward. But the marriage certificate showing Ward and Amalia Papadimos, twenty-three, a Greek citizen, in Las Vegas, was not convenient to Madonna.

She had *Evita.* She didn't have her man.

"I wish I were married and in a situation where having a child would be possible. People say, 'Well, have one on your own.' I say, 'Wait a minute, I'm not interested in raising a cripple.' I want a father there. I want someone I can depend on."

And, like Garbo, how long before she wants to be alone?

Madonna believes in fate. A fortune teller told her in 1991 that her heart would be broken, that she would not have children. That upset her. Then, the fortune teller told her that she was not suited

177

to her career choices. That devastated her. Madonna got drunk. For the first time in her life she lost control.

A story published in America said she had bought a crypt so she could be buried near Marilyn Monroe at Westwood Memorial Park. She hasn't done that. Yet.

Notes

Information about Madonna was derived from many sources. For Madonna's own words about her life and career, I have drawn upon the following:

David Ansen, "Madonna: The Magnificent Maverick," *Cosmopolitan*, May 1990.

David Ansen with Pamela Abramson, "Tracymania," *Newsweek*, June 25, 1990.

Carl Wayne Arrington, "Madonna," *People*, March 11, 1985.

Carl Wayne Arrington, "Madonna Sizzles," *US*, June 12, 1989.

John Blake, "Mr. Madonna, Can the Heart-breaker Hang Onto His Bride?" *Daily Mirror* (London), February 25, 1986.

Simon Bates, "Madonna Opens Her Heart," BBC (reprinted in the *Star*), January 13, 1987.

Chris Chase, "Madonna, the Material Girl and How She Grew," *Cosmopolitan*, July 1987.

Christopher Connelly, "Madonna Goes All the Way," *Rolling Stone*, November 22, 1984.

Barbara Foley, "Throughly Modern Madonna," *Los Angeles Times*, April 13, 1990.

Patrick Goldstein, "It's Not Easy Being Notorious," *Los Angeles Times*, May 5, 1991.

179

Lynn Hirschberg, "The Misfit," *Vanity Fair*, April 1991.

Stephen Holden, "Madonna Goes Heavy on Heart," *New York Times*, June 29, 1986.

Michael Kelly, "Playgirl of the Western World," *Playboy*, March 1991.

Simon Kinnersley, "The Girl Can't Help It," *Rolling Stone*, November 22, 1984.

Susanna Nicholson (compiler), "Loose Talk Special," *US*, July 11–25, 1988.

Glenn O'Brien, "Madonna!" *Interview*, June 1990.

Orion Pictures, press handout, 1985.

Forrest Sawyer, ABC News "Nightline," December 18, 1990.

Fred Schruers, "How's That Girl," *US*, September 7, 1987.

Kevin Sessums, "White Heat," *Vanity Fair*, April 1990.

Don Shewey, "The Saint, the Slut, the Sensation . . . Madonna," *Advocate*, May 7, 1991.

John Skow, Cathy Booth, Denise Worrell, "Madonna Rocks the Land," *Time*, May 27, 1985.

Elizabeth Sporkin, Sue Carswell, David Huchings, Lisa Russell, David Craig, John Griffiths, Jacqueline Savaiano, Lissa August, Georgina Oliver, "He Can Still Leave 'em Breathless," *People*, July 2, 1990.

Harry Dean Stanton, "Madonna," *Interview*, April 1985.

Benjamin Svetkey, "Some Like It Hot . . . Some Not," *Entertainment Weekly*, December 14, 1990.

Touchstone Pictures, *Dick Tracy* video promo, 1990.

Denise Worrell, "Now: Madonna on Madonna," *Time*, May 27, 1985.

Vicki Woods, "Madonna Holds Court," *Vogue*, May 1989.

and newspaper clipping, March 14, 1990, referring to the *Vanity Fair* interview and the David Letterman Show.